Essential
Egypt

by
NINA NELSON

Canadian-born Nina Nelson has wide experience as a
travel writer, and is the author of books on the Nile,
Hong Kong, Taiwan, Canada, Belgium, Malta
and Luxembourg.

Produced by AA Publishing

Written by Nina Nelson
Verified by Michael Haag
Peace and Quiet section
by Paul Sterry

Reprinted April 1999
Reprinted March 1998
Reprinted September 1997
Revised third edition 1997
Reprinted 1995 (twice)
Revised second edition 1995
Reprinted 1990
First published 1990

Edited, designed and produced
by AA Publishing.
© The Automobile Association
Maps © The Automobile
Association

Distributed in the United Kingdom
by AA Publishing, Norfolk House,
Priestley Road, Basingstoke,
Hampshire, RG24 9NY.

A CIP catalogue record for this
book is available from the British
Library.

ISBN 0 7495 1330 6

Published by AA Publishing, a
trading name of Automobile
Association Developments
Limited, whose registered office
is Norfolk House, Priestley Road,
Basingstoke, Hampshire,
RG24 9NY.
Registered number 1878835.

Colour Origination by: L.C. Repro
& Sons Ltd., Aldermaston,
England.

Printed by: Printers S.R.L., Trento
Italy.

Front cover picture: *Pyramids and
camel*

Contents

Country Distinguishing Signs

On some maps international distinguishing signs have been used to indicate the location of the countries which surround Egypt.

(IL) = Israel
(JO) = Jordan
(LAR) = Lybia
(SA) = Saudi Arabia
(SUD) = Sudan

This book employs a simple rating system to help choose which places to visit:

✓	'top ten'

◆◆◆ do not miss
◆◆ see if you can
◆ worth seeing if you have time

INTRODUCTION

The ancient Egyptians were one of the earliest civilised peoples on this planet. Back in the Old Testament days of Abraham, they possessed settled laws and an established government. Their country was as beautiful and unique as it is today: a shallow narrow valley of incredible fertility divided by the River Nile and edged by desert, bare hills and the Nile Delta.

The sun shines almost continually on the land, whose lifeblood is the Nile. Because the river, seemingly miraculously, rose each year, the Egyptians believed that in Paradise, aeons ago, the goddess Isis wept for her lost husband Osiris and her tears caused water to flow earthward into the Nile. During the annual flood, water overflowed the banks, left rich sediment for the crops and then subsided. Cities flourished along the river, aglitter with temples, statues, monuments, steles (carved tablets) of lapis lazuli, and obelisks whose summits shone with an overlay of gold and silver.

Succeeding rulers embellished the cities further and word of their magnificence spread. It was natural that when men developed the desire to travel they should be drawn to Egypt to see the wonders of Homer's hundred-gated city of Thebes, Elephantine Island, the holy city of Abydos, and Memphis, the ancient capital of Egypt. The great temples and tombs and the extraordinary pyramids along the valley of the Nile have, for the last 3,000 years at least, made Egypt a place of fascination for the traveller and a source of inspiration.

Without doubt, the thing that will strike the present-day tourist is the way the new blends with the old. Modern Cairo for instance, with its skyscrapers and television centre, rubs shoulders with ancient mosques, and the dark, narrow trading alleys of Khan el Khalili, where skilled craftsmen work as their forebears did. It is the same throughout the country. The old is as sharply divided from the new as is the Delta from the desert.

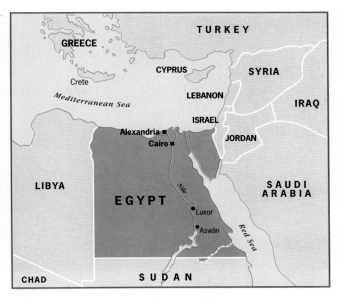

There are many places where the visitor can relax and play after sightseeing. The oasis of Faiyûm is a sportsman's paradise less than a morning's drive from Cairo; there are sunny beaches like Mersa Matrûh with its pale golden sand; and on the coast of the Red Sea opportunities for skin-diving and deep-sea fishing are second to none.

For inveterate sightseers, there is also Mount Sinai where Moses received the Ten Commandments and Alexandria with its catacombs, its Graeco-Roman museum displaying fine Tanagra figurines, and its famous beaches.

Most visitors will find something to their taste in Egypt. For the archaeologically-minded, it is *the* place for ancient monuments and ancient history; for those more interested in the present-day scene, there is the bustling city life of Cairo with exotic night spots and displays of folk dancing for entertainment, while the changeless pattern of peasant life continues along the Nile. Anyone interested in engineering must visit the Aswân Dam,

BACKGROUND

Egypt's heartblood: the flooded Nile, with the Colossi of Memnon. Engraving by David Roberts

and watersports enthusiasts will find no lack of deep sea fishing, snorkelling, scuba diving and windsurfing.

This book has been written for independent travellers as well as people on organised tours, but the novice may find it easier to join a tour, as there will be less uncertainty over prices, less hassle, and you will be sure of covering all the essential sights.

BACKGROUND

History of Ancient Egypt

The civilisation of Ancient Egypt grew out of several millennia of settlement in the Nile Valley, during which people gradually learned the skills of agriculture and of living in settled communities. By around 4000 BC some villages were growing stronger than others and their headmen began to control ever larger areas. These areas became the *nomes*, or administrative districts of Egypt. By about 3400 BC, two powerful kingdoms existed, one in the Nile Delta (Lower Egypt) and the other further south, in the Nile Valley (Upper Egypt). Legend has it that Narmer, or Menes, a king of

Upper Egypt, conquered Lower Egypt in about 3100 BC, bringing the whole country under his rule. This was symbolised by the creation of the royal double crown, combining the White Crown of Upper Egypt, which had a vulture emblem, with the Red Crown of Lower Egypt, which bore the emblem of a cobra. Narmer's victory is commemorated in his so-called 'palette', which is engraved with scenes of his exploits and with representations of the double crown. It can be seen in Cairo's Egyptian Antiquities Museum.

Around 280 BC Manetho, an Egyptian priest, divided his country's history into 30 dynasties, or royal families, from Menes to Alexander the Great. More recent historians have grouped these into the Old, Middle and New Kingdoms. During the so-called Pre-Dynastic period, some 300 years, the unity of Egypt was being consolidated and the political structure of the state laid down. By the time of the Old Kingdom (Dynasties III–VIII, about 2664–2155 BC), Egypt was a wealthy kingdom with its capital at Memphis. It had a highly developed art and architecture and an all-powerful ruler, the pharaoh. The pyramids, beginning with the Step Pyramid of Zoser at Sakkara and culminating in the great pyramids of Gîza, were built at this time, using a huge labour force and reflecting the wealth and power of the rulers.

By the Vth Dynasty, the position of the pharaoh was threatened by the increasingly powerful nobles and the influential priestly caste. This led to civil war and a period of political disintegration. Menhotep, a king of Thebes, finally reunited Egypt and ushered in the Middle Kingdom (XIIth Dynasty, about 2051–1786 BC), one of the most artistically accomplished and prosperous periods of Egyptian history. At home, great public works, such as the reclamation of the marshy Faiyûm region, were carried out, while abroad Egypt's armies conquered Nubia to the south and parts of Syria to the east. Decline came again as the pharaoh's authority weakened. Around 1700 BC, invaders called 'Hyksos' attacked northern Egypt. They were to dominate the country for about a hundred years. The south of Egypt, though not conquered by them, paid them tribute, and the Nubians gained the assistance of the Hyksos to recover their independence from Egypt. A positive side of the Hyksos' invasion was that the Egyptians encountered for the first time horses, chariots, spinning and weaving, and new musical instruments.

The city of Thebes was once again the source of Egyptian revival, with the rebellion led by Amasis, founder of the XVIIIth Dynasty which began the New Kingdom (Dynasties XVIII–XX, about 1554–1075 BC). This was Egypt's age of military power. Nubia was reconquered, and Syria, Palestine and parts of Mesopotamia came under Egyptian dominion. One of the rulers of the XVIIIth Dynasty was the female pharaoh Hatshepsut who ruled for 20 years, and was portrayed as a king with the pharaonic beard.

The most curious episode of the period was the reign of Amenhotep IV, who called himself Akhenaten. He tried to establish a monotheistic cult of the god Aten (the Sun-disk) and founded a new capital city near Amârna, Akhet-Aten, for his worship. It is possible that this was a political move to curb the excessive power of the priests of Amen-Ra at Thebes. There has been much speculation about the physical and mental condition of Akhenaten, based on the curious way he (and his family) are portrayed, with strange domed heads and elongated bodies. The crisis brought about by Akhenaten's action was resolved after his death, when his successor Tutankhamun moved the capital back to Thebes and restored the worship of Amen-Ra as the state religion. It was, of course, the finding of the undisturbed tomb of Tutankhamun in the Valley of the Kings at Thebes by archaeologists Howard Carter and Lord Carnarvon in 1922, that demonstrated to the world the incredible wealth with which pharaohs had been surrounded.

But other powerful forces were arising in the Middle East. The Hittites, from Asia Minor, became a danger, though Ramses II of the XIXth Dynasty managed to come to terms with them. A greater danger, however, were the so-called 'Sea People', wandering groups of raiders who, at the end of the 13th century BC, attacked the shores of the Mediterranean. Ramses III

The funeral mask of Tutankhamun, one of the priceless treasures found in the boy pharaoh's undisturbed tomb

(1182–1151 BC) of the XXth Dynasty finally conquered them in a great battle, at the mouth of the Nile. But the pharaohs gradually lost their authority and by about 1050 BC, Egypt's rule was divided between the high priest of Amen at Thebes and the vizier of Lower Egypt at Tanis in the northeast of the Delta, with the pharaoh ruler in name only.

There was a long period of anarchy during the XXIIIrd–XXVth Dynasties (about 760–650 BC). Indeed, the Nubians, formerly Egypt's vassals, themselves produced the pharaohs of the XXVth Dynasty. Then came invasions, first by the Assyrians (7th century BC), then by the Persians (6th century BC). The latter ruled Egypt with a firm hand for some 200 years.

From Alexander to Modern Egypt

Alexander the Great was welcomed as a liberator when he entered Egypt in 332 BC. On his death, Egypt again became an independent monarchy under Ptolemy, one of Alexander's generals. His dynasty ruled for 300 years. The predominant influence on official Egypt was now Greek. Alexandria, the new capital, became a brilliant centre of learning and art, and Greek replaced Egyptian as the state language. However, the Ptolemies wooed the natives to some extent by introducing a new religion combining elements of Greek and Egyptian worship, and encouraged the building of traditional Egyptian temples. The common people were probably largely untouched by Greek influence, maintaining their traditional customs and beliefs.

Next to occupy Egypt were the Romans after the battle of Actium in 31 BC and the death of the last Ptolemy, Cleopatra. Egypt was now governed by a prefect, solely responsible to the emperor Augustus who regarded the new acquisition as his personal property. The corn of Egypt fed Rome for centuries, but Egypt itself only grew poorer under the Romans. In AD 395 Egypt became part of the Eastern Roman Empire and so came under the domination of Byzantium. Christianity was embraced by many in preference to Roman religious customs, but the religious path of modern Egypt was set a few centuries later, when the Arabs invaded in 640. Byzantine power was swept away and the country gradually converted to Islam, so that today only a minority remains Christian – these are called Copts.

Now ruled by local governors under the Caliphs, Egypt became a powerful part of the Muslim world. The Fatimid dynasty founded a new capital, Cairo, in 969. In 1171 Saladin, founder of the Abbasid dynasty, became king of Egypt and initiated a series of conquests, bringing Syria, Mesopotamia and much of Arabia and North Africa under his power. After his death this empire rapidly disintegrated and, about 1250, the kingdom was taken over by the Mamelukes, a military group consisting of former Turkish and Circassian slaves who had once been royal bodyguards. When Egypt fell to the Turks in

1517 and became part of the Ottoman Empire, there had been some 250 years of settled and prosperous rule under the Mamelukes. Egypt declined under the Ottomans and sank into political obscurity. Napoleon was the next foreigner to lay claim to it, in 1798. The French occupation ended in 1801, and a powerful force now made itself felt in the person of a Turkish officer named Mohammed Ali, who soon became ruler and founded a dynasty. As Egypt's foreign debts mounted, however, France and Britain vied with each other for control, and Britain eventually imposed a protectorate. Even when this ended, in 1922, a British military presence was maintained for decades.

The last ruling king, Farouk, was forced to abdicate by a group of army officers in 1952 in favour of his infant son Fuad. In 1953 the officers abolished the monarchy and declared Egypt a republic. By 1954 Colonel Gamal Abdel Nasser had become prime minister and he led the country until his death in 1970. Latterly Egypt has been bedevilled by the Middle East wars with Israel, but the Camp David agreement, signed by Egypt's President Sadat and Israel's Prime Minister Begin under the auspices of American President Carter in 1979, produced more stability. Tourism, which has always flourished in Egypt and has been a pillar of the economy, especially since the days of the 'Grand Tour' at the turn of the century, is once again booming despite a setback after the Gulf War.

The bombardment of Alexandria in 1882 ushered in British rule in Egypt

Art and Architecture

In dynastic times those talented in any of the arts flourished as they never have before or since. They were held in veneration second only to the pharaoh himself. Pharaohs had among their splendid titles that of 'Scribe of the Sun' and nobles who could neither read nor write used the word 'scribe' as a distinguished appellation. Architects and artists were allowed unlimited gold to decorate monuments.

Senenmut, royal architect during the reign of Queen Hatshepsut, became one of the queen's chief advisers because of the magnificent temples he designed. The pharaoh Amenhotep III had an extremely gifted minister and architect, also named Amenhotep, who was venerated almost as a god and whose sayings were still being quoted 1,200 years after his death. Architecturally the pharaonic temples all followed a similar pattern. The temple was approached by a long avenue lined with stone figures (usually sphinxes) leading to an H-shaped entrance, with two flanking towers, or pylons, their sides slanting slightly inward. The entrance led to an open court edged on three sides by a colonnade. A vast pillared room, the

The Sphinx at Gîza, carved out of the natural rock about 4,500 years ago

hypostyle hall, lay beyond; this, in turn, led to chambers and passages. In the heart of the temple was the shrine where a figure of the god was jealously guarded. Inside the temple precincts was a sacred lake in which the royal barge was placed on special occasions and where the priests purified themselves before ceremonies. Except for statues, the only form of decoration in the temples were carvings on the walls and columns. In depictions of the pharaohs making suitable offerings to the gods, who give back in return strength, life and happiness, the figures are rigid, dignified and formal. These are in sharp contrast to the lively reliefs showing scenes from the royal daily life.

The visitor will notice that the figures are almost always in profile. In the few exceptions to this, the work is not of the same quality or even in proportion – for instance in the female form the breast is under the arm. In statues the left profile is more delicate than the right, the reason being that the sculptor only traced the left side of the face on the block and left the rest to be carved by his apprentices.

It is, paradoxically, in tombs that ancient Egypt springs colourfully to life. Here frescos modelled in low relief and painted in bright colours show scenes of everyday life on the river and in the fields as well as mysterious scenes of ritual.

Religion in Ancient Egypt

Pharaonic gods are many and difficult to catalogue. Some are replicas of each other and many have the same characteristics. As time passed, some deities assumed new roles and names while keeping their original character. Ra was the self-begotten great sun god, who became the state god Amen-Ra. His son, Osiris, was king of Egypt and ruled the land wisely until he was murdered by Set, his brother, who cut up his body and scattered it throughout Egypt. Osiris was resurrected thanks to his wife and sister Isis, who then gave birth to Horus. Horus became lord of the earth and Osiris god of the underworld and judge of the dead.

During religious ceremonies priests probably wore animal masks when representing gods, for each god not only possessed all human virtues but also a particular attribute of a bird or animal.

BACKGROUND

Egyptian Gods
Re, Ra Sun god, his bird head surmounted by a disc; father of Osiris.
Osiris Lord of the Underworld.
Isis Wife and sister of Osiris, who restored him to life after death; a kindly caring goddess.
Horus Hawk-headed son of Osiris and Isis; he reclaimed the throne from his father's murderer. Pharaohs identified themselves with him.
Hathor Cow-headed goddess of love and fun, similar to Aphrodite; wife and muse of Horus.
Anubis Dog-headed god of the dead.
Sobek Crocodile-headed god worshipped at Crocodilopolis, near Faiyûm city.
Sekhmet Feline-headed, vengeful goddess of war; also of doctors.
Bast Maternal cat-goddess.
Thoth Bird-headed Time Lord, who was also patron of scribes and, possibly was the layer of the cosmic egg.

Mummification

For the ancient Egyptian, life did not end when the body died. Elaborate funerary customs and rituals ensured for him a continued existence. The mummy – the embalmed body of a dead person – is the most familiar manifestation of this belief.

The macabre art of embalming reached its peak of perfection at Thebes. It was practised and known in Egypt for at least 5,000 years, and was discontinued only some 500 years after the birth of Christ. The people who carried out the work joined special guilds which were appointed by law.

Mummifying was performed in three different ways. The most skilful method, and therefore the most expensive, was by extracting the brain through the nose with a special iron probe without disfiguring the face in any way, and removing the intestines through the side after an incision had been made. The body cavity was filled with cassia, myrrh and other fragrant substances, then sewn together and immersed in natron (sesquicarbonate of soda) for 70 days in order to preserve the body. Afterwards it was carefully washed and wrapped in strips of fine linen smeared with gum. According to the

historian Diodorus this cost one talent of silver –
a huge sum in today's terms.

The second method was far less complicated.
The entrails were dissolved, the brain left in
place and the body again immersed in natron for
70 days. This cost half as much and dispersed all
save skin and bones.

The third way was most commonly used as it
cost little. A strong astringent was injected into
the body and it was salted for 70 days. If the
internal organs were mummified they were
separated, washed in palm oil and powdered
with aromatic herbs after which they were
sealed in four jars. One held the heart and the
others the liver and two intestines. The jars were
made of alabaster or terracotta and each was
inscribed. The gods to whom they were
dedicated protected them. These so-called
canopic jars were buried with the mummy
together with small *ushabti* figures, glazed
earthenware statues to assist the mummy in the
underworld.

Amulets were placed around the neck of the
dead, among them the papyrus sceptre,
emblem of the youth hoped for in the next
world; the vulture, ensuring the protection of
Isis; the key of life; and lastly the *utchat* in the
form of an eye which was the sign of good health
and happiness.

Other sacred things protected the body,
including scarabs, effigies of the deceased
adoring Osiris and models of the middle and
index fingers, representing the two fingers of
Horus stretched out to aid the dead. As soon as a
man died he became identified with Osiris, for it
was supposed that this god had been the first to
be embalmed and that Anubis had been head
embalmer.

It was believed that the dead traversed a long
lonely river called the Tuat before attaining the
glory of Ra. The Tuat, which was neither below
nor above the level of Egypt, had its source on
the west bank of the Nile, ran north, then bent
around to the east and ended where the sun
rose. It was divided into 12 parts beginning and
ending with a chamber. The name of the
entrance chamber was Amentet, and this was a
place of twilight. As the deceased continued the
awful journey the darkness became complete;

horrible monsters and reptiles rose from the
depths of boiling water. The last sections
gradually lightened until the final chamber was
reached.

Religion Today

The visitor cannot fail to notice that the Muslim
faith (Islam) is an important part of Egyptian life.
Aspects of it are not unlike Christianity, though in
many ways the two religions are very different.
The pages of the Koran, the Muslim holy book,
contain references to Abraham, Noah and
Moses, and Islam's founder Mohammed, who
was born some 500 years after Christ, studied
the life of Jesus and acknowledged the force of
his teachings as a prophet.

One difference between the two creeds is the
way the Muslim worships in public while the
Christian, except when in church, prays in
private. Five times a day, whether in a crowded
street or in the country, a devout Muslim will
unroll his prayer mat, or simply prostrate
himself on the bare ground, to make his
obeisance to God. The driver of your car may
draw up at the side of the road and ask you if
you will excuse him for a few minutes while he
says his prayers.

The words 'Allah is great and Mohammed is his
Prophet' are chanted from countless minarets
each day to remind the people of God. Each
believer is required to work out his own
salvation. According to a Muslim writer, Sayed
Ameer Ali: 'Each soul rises to its Creator without
the intervention of priest or hierophant. Each
human being is his own priest. In the Islam of
Mohammed no man is higher than another.'

Another difference between Christian and
Muslim is that the former tries to bend fate to his
will while the Muslim feels that everything is
preordained. Life has certain things in store for
him. He will try to place his footsteps one way
but if they diverge even slightly he knows that it
is God's will. God knows best. 'Elhamdo lel'Lah'
you hear on all sides in Egypt, meaning 'thanks
be to God'; or 'en sha Allah', if it is God's will'.
The latter is constantly used instead of saying
'yes'.

Ramadan is to the Muslim what Lent is to the
Christian, but the fast is far more stringent. It

begins when the new moon rises in the ninth
month of the Islamic year. From then, for 28 days,
a strict fast from dawn to sunset is observed. The
sick and ailing do not fast, neither do small
children or old people and there are various
conditions when there is dispensation for people
who would normally fast, for instance when
travelling.

A third difference between the two religions is the
way Christian graveyards are often neglected
while those of the Muslim are well kept. His burial
grounds resemble small villages with rounded
domes of white, pale blue or apricot. Many
Muslims save during their lives for such a resting
place so that when they are dead their children
and friends will visit their tomb on feast days, eat
there (unconsumed food is left for the poor) and
feel that once again they are together. Muslims
are very generous to the needy.

*Egypt's religion
today is the desert-
born faith of Islam.
Prayer is part of
everyday life as
shown in this
painting*

The Copts are the direct descendants of the
ancient Egyptians and are Christians. The Coptic
language fell into disuse after the Arab invasion
of Egypt during the 7th century, and since the
16th century, except for liturgical purposes, it

has been entirely replaced by Arabic. The Copts, some of whom living today bear an amazing resemblance to the figures carved on the walls of temples and monuments, were among the earliest Christians. In AD 64 Saint Mark ordained one Ananius patriarch of Alexandria and the city became the centre of Christianity. Two hundred years later Saint Anthony withdrew to the desert to abstain from worldly things, teaching his Christian followers to lead an ascetic life and so starting the first monastery.

The Copts are not subject to Rome, but make use of confession which is obligatory before receiving the Eucharist. The head of the Coptic Church, for centuries the patriarch of Alexandria, is now the patriarch of Cairo. His jurisdiction also extends over the Church in Abyssinia.

Coptic churches do not have organs. The only music allowed is cymbals and brass bells, the latter struck by a rod held in one hand. Religious representations take the form of icons in stiff Byzantine style, mostly portraying Christ in acts of benediction.

There are several Coptic legends, one of the most charming being that the Virgin Mary broke her fast when she arrived in Egypt by having a meal of dates. The cleft found in date stones is said to be the mark made by her teeth.

The People

Four fifths of Egypt's population are farming folk, the *fellaheen*. The Koran says, 'Man cannot exist without constant effort', and this is correct in their case. Irrigation and bright sunlight make the growth of crops so rapid that the *fellah* is constantly ploughing with his traditional yoke of buffalo or oxen, or gathering in his crops. His plough is made from a long tree trunk, the narrow end iron shod. The soil produces several crops annually. Indeed the clover the *fellah* grows to feed his animals, called *birseem*, produces greenery within a month; it is often easier to bring the animal to the food rather than gather it.

Clad in his long robe and skullcap, ploughing while white egrets (a protected species in Egypt) swoop at his heels to pick up insects, he

Nubische Häuptlinge bringen dem ägyptischen König ihre Geschenke. Um 1380 v. Chr. Wandgemälde in einem thebanischen Grabe des neuen Reiches (XVIII. Dynastie). Nach Le...

Nubian chiefs bring tributes to pharaoh in a tomb painting from Thebes of the 14th century BC

makes an attractive model for the photographer. Physically he is thin, and his sunburnt face with high cheek-bones may remind the onlooker of similar figures on temple walls. The *fellah's* womenfolk are equally photogenic when they wash their laundry on the river banks. Although the men wear traditional robes of white or pale striped cotton, the young women's dresses are vividly coloured, mostly in red and tangerine. Older women wear black. Completely different from the farmer, the present-day city dweller can be urbane and a linguist. There is great wealth and ability in the large towns. You will find Egyptian lawyers, surgeons, architects, archaeologists and business people throughout the world as well as in Egypt. Cairo today is a cosmopolitan city with every expected convenience available. Of course, after the expansion of the last two decades and now, with over 16 million inhabitants, the largest city in the Arab world, Cairo has its seamy side. Yet there are 5-star hotels, theatres, a modern opera house, a university, fine places of worship and other requisites of a capital city. Egyptians are naturally courteous, so much so that they will do anything to avoid arguments getting out of control, either among friends or with strangers. Their traditions of hospitality are famous.

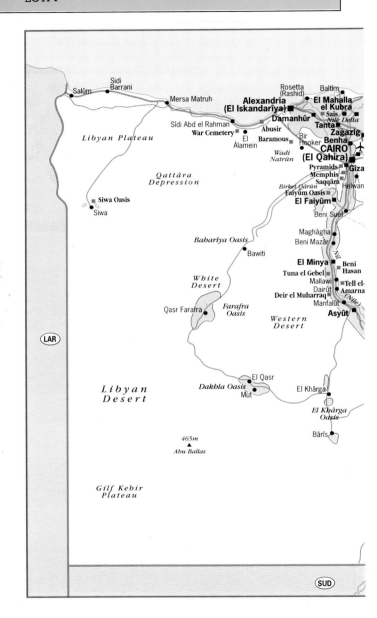

Salûm
Sidi Barrani
Mersa Matruh
Sîdi Abd el Rahman
Rosetta (Rashid)
Baltim
Alexandria (El Iskandarîya)
El Mahalla el Kubra
Damanhûr
Sais
Nile Delta
Tanta
Zagazig
Benha
CAIRO (El Qâhira)
Libyan Plateau
War Cemetery
Abusir
El Álamein
Baramous
Bir Hooker
Wadi Natrûn
Pyramids
Memphis
Saqqâra
Giza
Helwan
Qattâra Depression
Birket Qârûn
Faiyûm Oasis
El Faiyûm
Beni Suef
Siwa Oasis
Siwa
Maghâgha
Beni Mazâr
Baharîya Oasis
Bawiti
El Minya
Beni Hasan
Tuna el Gebel
Mallawi
Tell el-Amarna
Dairût
Deir el Muharraq
Manfalût
Asyût
White Desert
Qasr Farafra
Farafra Oasis
Western Desert
Nîl
Nile
(LAR)
Libyan Desert
El Qasr
Dakhla Oasis
Mut
El Khârga
El Khârga Oasis
465m
▲
Abu Ballas
Bârîs
Gilf Kebir Plateau
(SUD)

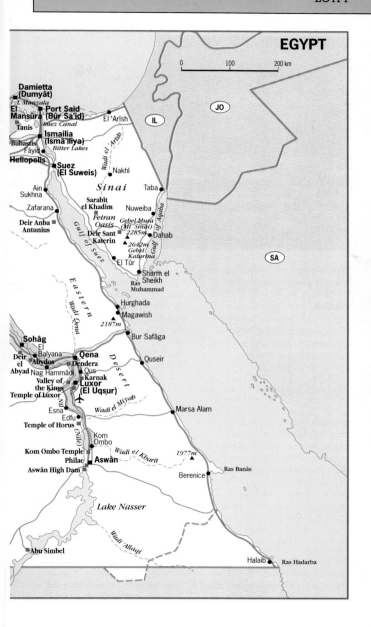

EGYPT

0   100   200 km

Damietta
(Dumyât)
L. Manzala
El   Port Said
Mansûra (Bûr Sa'id)
Tanis   El 'Arîsh
Ismailia   Suez Canal
(Ismâ'îliya)
Bubastis   Fâyid   Bitter Lakes
Heliopolis
Suez   Nakhl
(El Suweis)
Ain   Sinai   Taba
Sukhna
Zafarana   Sarabit   Nuweiba
el Khadim
Deir Anba   Feiran   Gebel Musa
Antunius   Oasis   (Mt Sinai)   Dahab
Deir Sant   2285m
Katerin   2642m
Gebel
Katarina
El Tûr
Sharm el
Ras   Sheikh
Muhammad

Hurghada
Magawish
2187m
Bur Safâga

Sohâg
El   Quseir
Deir   Balyana   Qena
el   Abydos   Dendera
Abyad Nag Hammâdi Qus
Valley of   Karnak
the Kings   Luxor
Temple of Luxor   (El Uqsur)
Esna   Marsa Alam
Edfu   Wadi el Miyah
Temple of Horus
Kom
Ombo
Kom Ombo Temple   Wadi el Kharit
Philae   1977m
Aswân
Aswân High Dam   Ras Banâs
Berenice

Lake Nasser

Wadi Allaqi

Abu Simbel   Halaib   Ras Hadarba

JO

IL

SA

Gulf of Suez

Gulf of Aqaba

Eastern

Wadi Qena

Desert

Nile

CAIRO

From the top of Cairo Tower there is a bird's-eye view of the city

CAIRO

Though more than a thousand years old, Cairo is yet young in historic Egypt. Today skyscrapers line the Nile, its main thoroughfare, criss-crossed with bridges bearing steady streams of traffic. On either side, streets are clogged with motorists who often keep their hands on their horns – unheeded by donkey carts and street vendors. There are women in western dress and high-heeled shoes and others in black robes and veils. Men throng the streets wearing suits or long cotton robes called *galabias*. All is movement and noise in this largest of African cities – population over 16 million. Yet you are made to feel part of it by the overall friendliness of the people. Often passers-by surprise you by smiling and saying 'welcome'. The best vantage point from which to see the city is the Cairo Tower on Gezira Island. It soars to some 600 feet (180m), and though made of reinforced concrete has an attractive open latticework exterior (12 million pieces of pottery were used in the design), which looks deceptively fragile, especially at night when it is floodlit. It casts its narrow shadow on Gezira Island, long known for its sporting club, the largest in the Middle East. The tower is encircled by its own garden where you will find chairs and tables for relaxing if you dislike heights. For those who wish to reach the top, a staircase of pink granite leads into the obelisk-like structure. The rounded walls of the entrance hall are studded with a series of mosaic pictures showing everyday life in modern Egypt. A lift whisks you upward and in a matter of seconds you are higher than the top of the

Great Pyramid. There is a revolving floor at the top from where you can see how the city spreads out from the Nile on both sides.

To the east is Garden City where there are several embassies, attractive villas and blocks of luxury flats. From here a tree-lined corniche leads out to **Maadi**, with its pleasant villas, flats and riverside fish restaurants, and then on to **Helwan** 18 miles (30km) distant, which used to be known as a spa but is now an industrialised town. However, it still has its attractive Japanese Gardens and health-giving sulphur baths can still be taken. Looking out from the tower you can glimpse mosques and slender minarets among the high buildings of the residential and commercial districts, sometimes traversed by tree-lined streets. Closer to hand is the modern section of Cairo and the many faculty buildings of Cairo University.

Immediately below, at the base of the tower, the Nile flows north. *Feluccas* rest in the lee of bridges or move silently over the water. The *felucca*, peculiar to Egypt, has a single sail with a very long yard so that it may catch each small gust of wind above the palm trees. They look as glamorous as gondolas and are as easy to hire. To the far west, lush greenery, sliced into small squares by blue irrigation channels, ends abruptly in dry sand. Huddled in the desert lie the great tawny Pyramids of Gîza.

Views from the tower at night are quite different. The bridges spanning the Nile appear as lines of pale amber light while from the heart of Cairo hectic neon signs pulsate on and off. The Mukattam Hills behind Saladin's famous Citadel now have a road curling up in a series of bends. There are several lookouts for motorists on the way up and from these you can look down on the tall minarets of the Mohammed Ali Mosque in the Citadel.

What to See in Cairo

◆◆
EL AZHAR MOSQUE AND UNIVERSITY
Shari El Azhar
This great institution is one of several monuments Cairo has inherited from the Fatimid Caliphs. The city did not bear the name Cairo until the time of the Fatimids who considered themselves direct descendants of Fatima, daughter of the Prophet Mohammed. They invaded Egypt from North Africa in AD 969 and foundations were laid for a walled city to house the Caliph. It was called El-Qâhira (The Triumphant), which we translate as Cairo – though the modern city has far outgrown its medieval confines.

High above the complex of buildings rise five minarets, each different. Only the mosque is open to the public. The original rectangular form of the building, begun in 970, is still the same though; after an earthquake in 1303, the mosque had to be rebuilt. Frequent restorations and additions have been made down the centuries but the character of the building has been preserved. Charity has

24

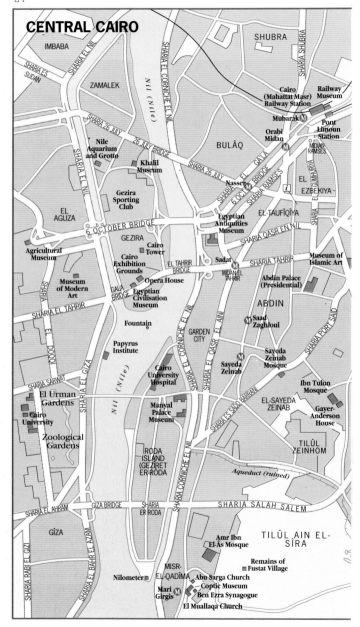

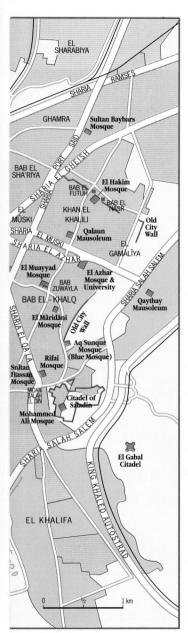

always been part of El Azhar's tradition: the blind were cared for, and even up to a century ago, hundreds of people would call on alternate days when bread and oil for lamps would be distributed.

It is a vast place, irregular in shape, with long avenues of columns, many from ancient buildings. Groups of students have their places reserved under niches and porticoes where they gather around their tutors. They remove their shoes and sit on carpets strewn over the stone floor. Tourists are asked to wear felt overshoes before they walk into the vaulted halls. The oldest *mihrab* (prayer-niche) is in a rectangular hall whose ceiling is supported by 140 columns. The library is remarkable, possessing 52,000 volumes of which 15,000 are

El Azhar mosque, 'The Splendid', is the heart of Islam's most important centre of learning

manuscripts, many priceless. In 980 the vizier (local governor), Yacub Ibn Killis, author of a highly regarded religious manuscript, took to reading aloud in the mosque. Because of this, other scholars thought it politic to do likewise. Finally several jurists were appointed to conduct religious studies there and so the university was born.

A thousand years later, El Azhar is paramount for Islamic learning. The old traditions continue. The rector and his staff wear the same type of robe that tutors have worn there from the beginning: dark blue *galabiehs* of fine wool and white turbans. Teaching is based on the Koran and students gather there from all over the Muslim world in their thousands. But modern studies can also be pursued today in nine faculties offering such subjects as medicine, law, engineering and agriculture. Some faculties are at Heliopolis on the outskirts of Cairo.

◆◆◆
COPTIC MUSEUM
Old Coptic Quarter
The Coptic Museum, part of which is built over the fortress next to the Hanging Church (see below), is reached through a garden with flower-covered pergolas and a fountain.
From earliest times Egypt exported textiles and cloth and in the museum you will see beautiful examples of wool and flax fabrics and tapestries from the 4th, 5th and 6th centuries (silks were very rare in those days). Their beautiful colours and intricate designs draw art

students looking for inspiration for lace and carpet making. Icons on display date from the 5th century and are all of religious themes.

Coptic Religious Art
The Copts avoided representing harrowing scenes of the torture of saints and martyrs, the Day of Judgement or the Devil, so that the icons have a pleasing gaiety and serenity.
Originally the paintings were made directly on the walls but, by the 11th century, because of frequent persecution of the faithful, they were painted on cloth, sheets of gold or ivory, so that they could be hidden when there was threat of war or pillage.
The Copts favoured floral or fruit designs; and many plants had a special religious value. For instance, Christ's words: 'I am the vine', led to the use of vine branches, leaves and clusters of grapes to embellish the capitals of columns, cornices and friezes. Palm fronds had been a sign of joy and welcome since pharaonic times and were freely used.

Woodwork exhibits are beautifully carved. The Copts carried on the art from dynastic days and the Muslims took it over from the Copts. One amusing carving, called 'Petition of Rats', shows three rats before a cat pleading for clemency and holding up a white flag. There is also a fine fresco from El-Faiyûm of Adam and Eve eating the apple in the Garden of Eden. Also on display is a bronze Roman eagle from the

Roman fortress of Babylon, which is the site of the most ancient part of Cairo. During the reign of Augustus it was used as the headquarters of one of the legions that garrisoned Egypt and parts of the Roman wall are still standing. *Open*: 09.00–16.00hrs; Friday 09.00–11.00hrs and 13.00–16.00hrs.

◆◆◆
EGYPTIAN ANTIQUITIES MUSEUM ✓

north of Tahrir Square
This is the richest museum of Egyptian antiquities in the world. It contains pharaonic treasures going back 5,000 years and is open daily. The building is rectangular with a large rotunda on the ground floor containing massive exhibits including colossal statues of Ramses II. The best views of them can be obtained looking down from the upper galleries. Many of these have skylights. The exhibits displayed in glass cases are usually placed on white linen, a material always associated with ancient Egypt. Inevitably, the gold and alabaster trappings from the tomb of Tutankhamun draw the crowds and there are people whose sole reason for visiting Egypt is to see them. If you have little time to spare, turn right at the entrance and you can ascend a stairway to the special gallery.

Crossing the threshold of the Tutankhamun Gallery you walk between two man-size figures made of ebony. Golden skirts encircle their loins, sandals of gold are on their feet and above proud foreheads they wear golden head-dresses. They stand at the alert, each man holding a staff topped with a golden ball. They were to guard the pharaoh's tomb. The gallery is

Centrally situated, the Egyptian Antiquities Museum is a 'must'

Varied and amazing exhibits: mummified body of Ramses II...

high with grey walls, diffused light coming from skylights in the roof.

All the trappings of court life are here: golden chariots, fabulous golden furniture, chairs, chests, divans, beds. Nowhere else in the world can so much gold be seen. Small golden figures displayed in glass cases depict scenes from the life of Tutankhamun in individual tableaux. Many portray dramatic incidents such as the king about to harpoon a crocodile. Others represent happenings from the royal daily life. One glass case contains a gilded wooden shrine to Tutankhamun defended on each of its four sides by goddesses, their arms outspread along the walls.

Music was a part of court life as can be seen by the slender trumpets and lutes. There are many perfume vessels of alabaster; one, a rounded jar, has a minute tiger as a handle, his small red tongue hanging out, his fur tawny striped, looking so freshly painted it is impossible to believe it was made some 3,000 years ago.

Many of the Tutankhamun tomb treasures have been on display in museums round the world, even the golden mask. Yet one exhibit has always remained in Cairo, the famous statue of Anubis, god of the dead. This lifesize ebony jackal, his gold-lined ears cocked, his golden collar taut about his neck, stares at the entrance, the whites of his eyes showing. Like the Sphinx his haunches are close to his side, paws forward. He waits alert yet peaceful on his golden shrine. He is so thin that his rib cage shows. When the

archaeologist Howard Carter first found the tomb, a shawl was tied about the statue's shoulders as if to ward off the cold. Other exhibits not to be missed include the famous carved palette of Narmer (ground floor), dating from the very beginning of Egyptian history more than 5,000 years ago; the diorite statue of Chephren (Room 42); the painted limestone double statue of Rahotep and Nefret (Room 32); and the mysterious relics of the reign of Akhenaten, so different from the rest of dynastic art. The Mummy Room has about a dozen regal mummies from the Valley of the Kings, including those of Seti I and his son Ramses. The gallery is kept in semi-darkness so that visitors can experience the atmosphere of the original tombs. There is an additional charge to enter. If possible, visit this museum early in your stay, as it is likely that you will want to make a second visit.
Open: 09.00–16.00hrs; Friday 09.00–11.15hrs and 13.30–16.00hrs.
Entrance charge; extra fee for Mummy Room and cameras.

...4,500-year-old aristocratic couple, Rahotep and Nefret

GAYER ANDERSON HOUSE
next to Ibn Tulun Mosque
Of historic houses open to the public this is probably the best known. During the 17th century two neighbouring traditional houses were made into one when their top floors were joined together. Over 60 years ago the house was bought and restored by an Englishman, Major Gayer Anderson, a great collector of works of art and antiques, both western and oriental. He lived

there for many years and when he died in 1942 he bequeathed both house and contents to the Egyptian government for the most charming of reasons – in recognition of the years of happiness he had spent there. The house is attractive even on the outside where there are overhanging *mushrabia* (wooden latticework) balconies and shutters. There is a sunken mosaic fountain in the centre of a drawing room and high up in the reception rooms there are *mushrabia* screens through which the women sitting in galleries could watch what was going on below without themselves being seen. The delicately carved wood appears almost like fine lace as you look through it. There are hidden doorways, a beautiful statue of

Bast, the cat goddess, gilded icons, and some paintings – one of Anderson himself shows his features superimposed on the head of the Sphinx.

The Gayer Anderson House is administered by the Islamic Art Museum and one entrance ticket covers both museums.

◆◆
HANGING CHURCH
Old Coptic Quarter
The 'Hanging Church', or El Muallaka, dates back to the 7th century, though there may have been a church here as early as the 4th century. The building spans two bastions of a Roman city gate, so that the entrance is up some 25 marble steps; when you look out of the windows, instead of seeing the ground you look down into a deep Roman moat – hence the name Hanging Church. Having scaled the staircase you find yourself in a screened portico. Through a door in the back there is a small cloister and this leads into the church itself. On the right is an ancient painting of the Virgin and Child, and it seems as though the Virgin's eyes follow you as you move about. On the same wall there is an icon of Saint Mark. One of the treasures is a carved wooden panel of the Nativity from the 10th century.

The Holy Child lies in a manger from which two animals are eating, while the Virgin sits by the manger, which is carved with Coptic crosses.

◆◆◆
IBN TULUN MOSQUE
off Shari Darb El Hosr
This is said to be Cairo's oldest mosque and differs from any other in having a spiral minaret with a winding staircase outside leading to a gallery on top. The mosque's open court is square and measures 300 feet (90m) across. It is surrounded by cloisters on three sides, each consisting of two rows of columns. On the fourth, which faces Mecca, there are five rows. A domed fountain lies in the centre of the court.

The builder of the mosque was Ahmed Ibn Tulun, founder of the Tulunid dynasty, which ruled Egypt from 870 to 904. He has been remembered for centuries because of his striking mosque which, along with that of Sultan Hassan, is the finest in Cairo. The mosque is reached by walking up a slope, going through some doors and up a further slope and then climbing a short flight of steps before entering the mosque itself. At once you are aware of the quietness after the noisy street.

◆◆◆
ISLAMIC ART MUSEUM
Ahmed Mahir Square
Visitors interested in Islamic art should not miss this museum. Precious objects now displayed there were brought from other mosques and monuments and stored in the mosque of El Hakim for many years. They were eventually put on display in the present museum, sharing the building with the National Library. Recently the latter has been removed and the additional space has proved invaluable. The museum has one of the world's most important collectionsof Islamic art and

The 9th-century Ibn Tulun mosque, an architectural treasure

Photography
A small fee, in addition to admission charges, is sometimes required to take photographs at tourist sites. Be careful not to point your camera at military bases, and always, out of courtesy, ask permission to photograph the locals.

covers every aspect, including ceramics, fabrics and glass (note the fine collection of mosque lamps). The wooden panels from the Fatimid caliphs' palace at Fustat, the first place in Egypt to be settled by the Arabs, can also be seen. They show scenes from court life including hunting and music. More finds from Fustat include fresco paintings and carpet fragments.

In the Koran collection the oldest parchment dates back to the 8th century. The museum's earliest tombstone with Kufic (early Arabic) writing comes from the Nile valley. Room 20 is hung with marvellous prayer carpets. One of black brocade with silver threads, displayed under glass, used to be carried by camel to Mecca annually at the time of the Pilgrimage.
Open: 09.00–16.00hrs; Friday 09.00–11.00hrs and 14.00–16.00hrs.

◆◆◆
MOHAMMED ALI MOSQUE ✓

in the Citadel
The great stone fortress known as the Citadel was started in 1176 by the great sultan and opponent of the Crusaders, Saladin. Historians claim that it was built with the blocks from the smaller Pyramids at Gîza. Within its precincts is the alabaster-faced Mosque of Mohammed Ali which dates from the early part of the 19th century.
Mohammed Ali, after whom the mosque is named, was born in 1769 (the same year as Napoleon and Wellington) and came to Cairo as a Turkish officer. In 1806 he made himself ruler of Egypt within the Ottoman Empire and ruled Egypt for 43 years. In 1811 he invited his adversaries, the remaining Mameluke princes (members of a military body who had seized the throne of Egypt in 1254) to a banquet with the request that they should parade in front of the Citadel. Resplendent in magnificent

CAIRO

The ornate Mohammed Ali mosque dates from the last century

uniforms and seated on richly caparisoned steeds they rode into the courtyard. The portcullis was lowered and from every corner musketry fire was opened on them, continuing until all but one were dead. He escaped by leaping his horse over the wall – or so the story for tourists goes. The mosque forms two adjacent squares, one being the open courtyard fringed with domed porticoes, the other the great prayer-hall with its huge dome supported by four pillars and bordered by four semi-cupolas. Built in accordance with Ottoman taste, it is both criticised and praised. It has been said to be too ornate, poor in design, too ostentatious to be in keeping with the Muslim tradition. Admirers, on the other hand, have described it as one of the most magnificent of all mosques, and certainly it lends a note of splendour to the Cairo skyline.

Before entering you pull slippers over your shoes so as not to profane the prayer hall. Once inside you are immediately conscious of the hovering dome. Beneath, there is a vast emptiness save for the tomb of Mohammed Ali which is next to the pulpit where the Koran is read. Underfoot the carpet stretches to walls of smooth honey and white alabaster. Overhead are hundreds of suspended lamps which, when switched on, flood the mosque with subdued light. Outside in the courtyard, on a small tower, stands what is called the 'Gingerbread Clock', though nobody knows why. It was given to Mohammed Ali by King Louis Philippe of France in 1846 in exchange for the obelisk presented to France by the Egyptian ruler and which now stands in the Place de la Concorde in Paris, on the site of the infamous guillotine.

◆◆◆
THE OPERA HOUSE
Gezira Island
In 1971 when preparations were in hand for the celebration of the centenary of the first performance of Verdi's opera *Aida*, the Cairo Opera House was burnt down. The fire started on the top floor and hundreds of people gathered in Opera Square as the news spread. Despite the efforts of firemen to get the flames under control, the Opera House, with all its equipment, scenery and costumes, was completely destroyed. It was not until late 1988 that, phoenix-like, a new Opera House appeared, built with a $50 million grant from Japan. Materials came from various countries: marble from Italy, glass from the former Czechoslovakia and wood from Scandinavia. The carpets were woven in Egypt. Over the auditorium is suspended a fibreglass ceiling with a beautiful lotus design, the Japanese signature. The main auditorium has seating for 1,200, a smaller one holds 1,000 and there is an outdoor theatre holding 600.

◆◆
RIFAI MOSQUE
Shari El Qa'la
This is opposite the Mosque of Sultan Hasan (see below) near the Citadel and is one of Cairo's most modern mosques having been completed only in 1910 by Khedive Abbas II (ruler of Egypt at the time). Within its precincts are the tombs of the recent kings of Egypt. The late Shah of Iran is also interred there awaiting return to his own country in due course. Its hand-carved *minbar* (pulpit) is studded with mother of pearl and ebony and the carpets are exquisite in colouring and design.

◆
SAINT BARBARA'S CHURCH
Old Coptic Quarter
The Church of Saint Barbara, founded in the 5th century, contains a small chapel to Saint George and has some delightful murals. You will be shown a reliquary said to contain a bone of Saint Barbara, who suffered martyrdom in about 235.

◆◆
SAINT SERGIUS (ABU SERGA) CHURCH
Old Coptic Quarter
Vying with the 'Hanging Church' (see above) for the title of Cairo's oldest church, St Sergius stands at the end of a narrow alley. The crypt is supposed to be the exact place where the Holy Family sheltered for a month after their flight to Egypt. Some parts of the church go back to the 5th century, but it was rebuilt in the 11th century. The crypt measures 20 by 15 feet (6m by 4m) and is bare save for some marble pillars and a small recess.

The church itself is small and oblong with three altars on the east side, each in its own chapel. The pulpit is of rosewood inlaid with ebony and ivory. Another interesting point is that 11 of the columns in the nave are of streaked white marble while the twelfth is made of Aswân granite.

◆◆◆
SULTAN HASAN MOSQUE
Shari El Qa'la
Situated at the foot of the Citadel is the enormous Mosque of Sultan Hasan, built between 1356 and 1393 and regarded by many as the most beautiful in the Middle East. The entrance is imposing, springing upward like a Gothic arch, surrounded by honeycomb tracery, culminating in a shell design. Of the two remaining minarets the southern one is the loftiest in Cairo soaring to 267 feet (85m). The open courtyard within the building is immense with a richly decorated fountain in the centre. The dome over the mausoleum is 181 feet (55m) high, the highest in any Islamic monument. The elevated chair from which the Koran is read stands on eight slender pillars, a bronze door near by is inlaid with damascene work in gold and silver and the richly carved *minbar* (pulpit) is of special interest to tourists. You are told that if you make a wish while walking beneath it your request will be granted.

◆
SYNAGOGUE BEN EZRA
Old Coptic Quarter
Beyond the churches of Saint Sergius and Saint Barbara (see above), you will come upon a Jewish synagogue, the oldest in Egypt. Once a Coptic church, it was sold to the Jews by Michael, a patriarch, towards the end of the 9th century. It has now been restored to its full splendour, though its Jewish community disappeared long ago.

Accommodation
Cairo is well endowed with hotels, many of which come up to modern luxury standards. Some special recommendations are described below.
Atlas Zamalek, Mohandesseen (tel: 02 3464175). Located away from downtown but close to popular restaurants and shops. There is a pool and roof-top restaurant. 4-star
Cairo Marriott, Shari el Gezira, Zamalek (tel: 02 3408888). The hotel has been created from Khedive Ismail's 19th-century palace which he had built for the opening celebrations of the Suez Canal. The apartments intended for the Empress Eugénie, who was to be a guest, were designed as a replica of those she occupied in the Tuileries in Paris. The original palace is now flanked by two tower blocks of bedrooms. Part of the formal gardens have made way for tennis courts, swimming pool and health clubs. 5-star
Cairo Sheraton Gala Square, Dokki, (tel: 02 3488600). On the second floor there is an outdoor sun deck and circular heated swimming pool. The dining room at the top offers a sweeping vista out to the Pyramids. 5-star
Club Méditerranée, Le Manial (tel: 02 844524). Situated on the island of Roda. Accommodation is in air-

conditioned twin-bedded bungalows with shower room. 4-star

Concorde Hotel, 146 Shari El Tahrir, Dokki (tel: 02 708751). Situated near Cairo Airport with a complimentary bus service between the hotel and the city centre. There is a swimming pool and tennis court and rooms have television and minibar. 3-star

El Borg, Shari el Gezira (tel: 02 3406179). Across the Nile from Shepheard's Hotel close to the Cairo Tower. The Andalusian Gardens and a small obelisk are near by. 3-star

El Nil, 12 Shari Ahmed Ragab, Garden City (tel: 02 3542800). Near the British Embassy and Meridien Hotel and within walking distance of the American Embassy. 3-star

Flamenco, 2 El Gezira El Wosta, Zamalek (tel: 02 3400815). Offers two restaurants and lounge, pastry shop, bookstore, bank, travel agency and business centre. 4-star

Gezira Sheraton, Gezira Island, (tel: 02 3411555). This new Sheraton on Gezira Island is quite close to the older one on the west bank. Both have marinas on the Nile. This one is a 27-floor circular tower. The top eight floors offer exclusive suites with their own reception desk and lift. 5-star

Horus House, 21 Shari Ismail Mohamed, Zamalek (tel: 02 3403977). A pleasant pension-type hotel, often recommended. 3-star

Meridien Le Caire, Corniche el Nil (tel: 02 3621717). The hotel is superbly sited on Roda Island. From one side of it you have the impression that you are on a river boat. There are three

Cairo's palatial Marriott Hotel once played host to France's Empress Eugénie

restaurants as well as a snack-bar, a nightclub and two swimming pools. 5-star

Nile Hilton, Tahrir Square (tel: 02 765666). The main restaurant is built with two-level seating so that every guest may have a view of the Nile and, if it is not hazy, the Gîza Pyramids. There are self-contained apartments on the top floor, a shopping arcade and outdoor pool in the garden. The Egyptian Antiquities Museum is next door. 5-star

Ramses Hilton, Corniche el Nil (tel: 02 754999). This is one of the tallest buildings in Cairo with 36 floors. It is within walking distance of the Egyptian Antiquities Museum and shopping streets. There are luxury suites with galleried bedrooms and it has one of the few underground garages in Cairo. 5-star

Safir Cairo, 4 El Missaha Square, Dokki (tel: 02 3482424). Situated 10 minutes from the centre and 45 minutes from the airport. Banqueting facilities, pool and health club. 4-star

Safir El Zamalek, 21 Mohammed Mazhar, Zamalek (tel: 02 3420055). Offers three restaurants and bar. Beauty/barber shop. 5-star

Semiramis Inter-Continental, Corniche el Nil (tel: 02 3557171). Built over the site of the old Semiramis Hotel, famous as British HQ during World War II, it has wonderful views over the Nile and city. Recreational facilities include outdoor pool and bar. 5 star

Helnan Shepheard's, Corniche el Nil (tel: 02 3553900). This hotel's predecessor in the middle of Cairo was one of the world's

most famous from the turn of the century until after World War II. Close to Cairo's main attractions, it has 281 rooms, with restaurants, bars, coffee shop, night club, health club, ballroom and meeting facilities. 5-star

Sonesta, 4 Shari El Tayaran, Nasr City (tel: 02 2628111). Convenient for the airport, a small luxury hotel complete with business centre and swimming pool. Limousine service to the airport. A member of the Golden Tulip Group. 5-star

Windsor Hotel, 19 Shari Mohammed Bey el Alfi (tel: 02 915277). One of the more moderately priced small hotels but conveniently situated downtown; 55 rooms. 3-star

Nightlife and Entertainment

The big hotels usually have their own discos and often a nightclub and/or casino. Belly dancing is, of course, the standard entertainment in the nightclubs. There are numerous Arab nightspots along the Pyramids Road offering Middle Eastern singing and dancing. For history without tears, *son et lumière* shows can be seen at the Pyramids.

Restaurants

International cuisine is available in the restaurants of hotels and there are often snack-bars and pizzerias also attached to hotels. A few restaurants offering a more individual gastronomic experience are listed below.

Andrea, off the Pyramids Road (tel: 02 851133). Specialises in chicken on the spit.

Arabesque, Shari Qasr el Nil (tel: 02 5748677). Middle Eastern cuisine in an authentic setting.

The Farm, off the Pyramids Road
(tel: 02 851870). Specialises in
grilled fish and lamb.
Groppi, Shari Abdel Khaliq
Sarwat (tel: 02 5743244). Well-
known Cairo institution
established in 1890 and famous
for ice cream.
Khan el Khalili restaurant at
5 El Badistan Lane (tel: 02
903788). Here you will find a
very quiet and unusual place
where you can relax in small
rooms. They lead off a narrow
passageway, dimly lit through
mushrabia screens, and have a
Victorian ambience.

*Shoppers looking for souvenirs and
gifts can explore markets like Khan
el Khalili (right) or buy their own
'antiquity' (below)*

Nile Pharaoh Cruising Restaurant, Gîza (tel: 02 726122). Cruise up and down the river while you eat.

Shopping

It is not so easy these days to find authentic craftware, but in Khan el Khalili (see below) it is still possible to unearth something genuine from beneath all the tourist souvenirs on offer. For those seeking high quality shopping, Cairo also has modern shopping centres and luxury shops.

Karnak Bazaar. Close to the Corniche el Nil, near the new Shepheard's and new Inter-Continental hotels and facing the US Embassy you will find Karnak Bazaar. It reaches back almost to the Corniche and is a fascinating emporium. One side of it has a façade decorated with pharaonic-style carvings which, although the work of modern craftsmen, proves that they have lost none of the skills of their forebears. Within you will find Egyptian ornaments beautifully lit and displayed, ivory figures, antiques, translucent alabaster goblets, statues of gods and goddesses, brass and copper vases inlaid with silver. There are engraved Islamic lamps, plates, gold and silver jewellery and priceless rugs.

Khan el Khalili. The original Khan, or bazaar, was built in 1382 by Amir Garkas el Khalili, hence the name. The streets are mostly too narrow for traffic and sometimes even roofed over. Some of the shops are quite large while others are open-fronted stalls where you can often see craftsmen at work on brass and leather. There is much bargaining and drinking of coffee and it pays to look around before buying anything in order to get the feel of the place. There are gold and silver filigree work, lovely fabrics, scents and jewellery. You can have a *galabieh* (robe) made to special order in one or two days.

At **Agati** and some other silversmiths you can buy traditional silver sets for dressing or dining tables more cheaply than in Europe, because silver is sold by weight. The making of amber necklaces is fascinating to watch. When polished they are smooth to the touch and Muslims buy strings of them to carry and slide through their fingers as they whisper the various names of Allah.

Onnig of Cairo, Egyptian Antiquities Museum. Some of Onnig's replicas of pharaonic treasures are sold in the British Museum in London and the United Nations building in New York, but his most beautiful objects are in his shop at the Egyptian Museum, close to the front entrance. A member of the American Gemological Society, he has in his office many photographs taken with famous personalities. Onnig specialises in replicas and jewellery.

Shopping centres. Several of the larger hotels have shops in their foyers, while both Hiltons have much larger shopping enclaves if you do not want to wander far afield or are short of time. They sell clothing, shoes, souvenirs, food, cameras and radios. Similar goods can be bought in the luxury suburb of Heliopolis, about 6 miles (10km) from the centre of Cairo.

Urban sprawl is eclipsed by the majesty of the Pyramids at sunset

EXCURSIONS FROM CAIRO

GÎZA

Gîza, with its most famous attractions, the Pyramids, is surprisingly near to Cairo, only 7½ miles (12km) from the centre. It can be reached by bus, but it is more convenient to take a taxi. For centuries the first sights on the list of travellers to Egypt have been the Pyramids and Sphinx: fortunately they are close together. The road leading to them today is lined with blocks of flats, hotels, villas and nightclubs. Down its centre the old tram line has been replaced by green topiary. As you approach, there is the sudden surprising appearance against the sky of the Great Pyramid of Cheops to the left. Behind it, but not seen from this angle, are the two smaller ones of the Gîza group built later – one for the son of Cheops, Chephren, and the other for Mycerinus, Chephren's successor. Chephren built his pyramid next to his father's to the southwest. It is somewhat smaller but still retains some of its original casing.

These great monuments date from the middle of the 3rd millennium BC.

There is an admission charge for the Pyramids themselves.

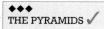

◆◆◆
THE PYRAMIDS ✓

The Great Pyramid
The Pyramid of Cheops is the only survivor of the Seven Great Wonders of the Ancient World and it can be seen in a variety of ways. You can go by private car, taxi or bus or stop at a camel 'garage' a quarter of a mile below it and continue from there by various means of transport. You can walk, take a pony and trap, ride a horse or, as most people prefer, take a camel. The size of the largest pyramid is awe-inspiring as you approach it more closely. It is 450 feet (137m) high and measures 754 feet (230m) along each side. Remember it was built with none of the mechanical aids we know today, but entirely by manual labour. Walk along the base, consider the size and number of the blocks (nearly 2.5 million) and you start to feel like an ant. You can enter the central chamber, but climbing the slopes is no longer allowed. Like all the pyramids, it was built as a tomb, the shape possibly intended to help the spirit of the dead pharaoh to rise to heaven. *Open*: 08.00–16.30hrs.

Pyramid of Chephren
This is the best preserved of the three main Gîza Pyramids and is only slightly smaller than the Great Pyramid. The top part still retains the original facing of smoothly finished stone, giving an idea of how the pyramids would originally have appeared. You can enter the main burial chamber along a steep passage, but take a guide.

Pyramid of Mycerinus
Smaller than the other two, the pyramid's lower courses were dressed with pink granite, but the upper part of the pyramid's casing was never completed. You can visit the burial chambers 20 feet (6m) below ground. Three smaller pyramids, one of which belonged to Mycerinus' wife, can be seen near by.

◆
PHARAONIC VILLAGE
A few years ago Dr Hassan Ragab, an ex-diplomat whose hobby is Egyptology, revived the

Moses in the bulrushes: one of the tableaux vivants *in Dr Ragab's Pharaonic Village*

craft of making papyrus, the ancient paper manufactured from an aquatic plant growing along the Nile banks and which had not been used for nearly a thousand years. More recently he has taken his researches into Egypt's past further and has built a Pharaonic Village on an island in the Nile at Gîza. You sit in a barge which is towed along canals past a succession of *tableaux vivants* showing many of the occupations of ancient Egypt, while a commentary is given. You can see planting and sowing, reaping of crops, bee-keeping, boatbuilding, even a re-enactment of Moses in the bulrushes. There are good opportunities for photographers,

especially when you go ashore into a village at the end of the tour. A visit lasts two hours (*open*: daily, 09.00–16.00hrs).

Dr Ragab's **Papyrus Institute**, which can also be visited, is on a boat on the river not far from the Cairo Sheraton Hotel. Here and in the Pharaonic village, hand-painted pictures on papyrus make easily packed souvenirs, and can be mailed anywhere in the world (*open*: 10.00–19.00hrs).

◆◆◆
SOLAR BOAT MUSEUM

On the southern side of the Great Pyramid, this small museum houses a boat found in a so-called 'boat pit' near the pyramid. It was excavated in 1954 by the Egyptologist Kamal el Mallakh, who had suspected its presence. When unearthed it was discovered to have been dismantled for storage. The dry atmosphere within the chamber had preserved the timbers and ropes almost perfectly. It was painstakingly reassembled and eventually housed in the special air-conditioned museum behind the pyramid.

The boat resembles a giant gondola about 150 feet (45m) long, its timbers made from cedars of Lebanon. The central cabin even demonstrates elementary air-conditioning, being fitted with a double-skinned roof.

Some of the oars and fittings look as if they had been made yesterday. It was believed that the boat would take the *ka* or soul of the pharaoh through the dark river of death to eternal light and rebirth.

Open: daily, 09.00–14.00hrs.

EXCURSIONS FROM CAIRO – GÎZA

The Gîza Pyramids and the Sphinx: number one tourist attraction

◆◆◆
THE SPHINX

The Sphinx, carved out of a natural rocky outcrop, is close to the Pyramid of Chephren, its expression patient and wholly mysterious. It is said that, 3,733 years before Christ, its body lay hidden by sand but its head gazed out over the desert and the Nile. Tuthmosis IV in the 15th century BC cleared away the sand and again, in 1905, the haunches and great paws were excavated. The lion's body stretches 150 feet (45m) and the paws are 50 feet (15m) long, the head 30 feet (10m) long and 14 feet (4m) wide, yet the Sphinx is small in comparison to the vast hulks of the Pyramids. It is not known who created it. Unfortunately the soft stone has been badly damaged since the Sphinx was unearthed. The Turks are said to have used it for target practice and wind and sand have also blasted pieces away. Now it is fenced off and you can no longer get as close to it as you might wish. The *son et lumière* has added immeasurably to the fascination of the monuments. The Pyramids seem to be coated once again in smooth sandstone and the Sphinx's features look whole. Performances are usually fully booked and the commentary is in different languages each night so it is important to check both before you go. Sunset, when there are not too many sightseers about, is a good time to see this unique scene and there is a wonderful view over Cairo from the plateau on which the monuments stand.

Accommodation

Green Pyramids, 13 Helmiat, El Ahram Street, El Ahram (tel: 02 537619). Tucked away off the Pyramids Road out of Cairo, this hotel grew out of an idea of Dr Yussef Wahby, a famous actor who, on retirement, decided to build a Swiss villa in an Egyptian setting. The result was a lavishly furnished house that might have arrived by magic carpet from a Swiss Alp. Wahby missed his friends and audiences and solved his problem by letting hoteliers build a hotel round his own villa. Three new bedroom blocks have been squeezed into the landscaped gardens of the villa and somehow seem to fit in with the original concept. There are also deluxe baroque suites, a poolside restaurant and the Bodega, a chalet type restaurant with a rustic interior offering international and Swiss specialities at any time of the day. 4-star

Holiday Sphinx, Alexandria Desert Road, Gîza (tel: 02 854700). Close to the Gîza Pyramids with a good view of them. Swimming pool and attractive garden. Near the Mena House Oberoi and Jolieville hotels. 4-star

Jolieville Hotel, Alexandria Desert Road, Gîza (tel: 02 3852555). Operated by the Swiss group Mövenpick and built on one level. Excellent cuisine.

Provides a bus service into Cairo. Speciality restaurants and souvenir shop. 5-star

Mena House Oberoi Hotel, Pyramids Road, El Ahram (tel: 02 3833222). This luxury hotel is built on a site that no other hotel can boast – facing the Great Pyramid of Gîza. It was originally the Royal Lodge of Khedive Ismail who used it as a guest house for friends visiting the Pyramids. It was enlarged into a luxury hotel. Antiques were bought from various towns in Egypt, including screens and furniture with *mushrabia*, exquisitely cut wooden lattice-work inlaid with ivory and mother of pearl. When hotel balconies were unheard of, each bedroom at Mena House had an open balcony leading from french windows so that guests could enjoy having their breakfast out of doors if they wished. The swimming pool, believed to be the first in any hotel, was a large marble one, refilled daily with fresh water. Oberoi Hotels have refitted the deluxe rooms and suites with minibars, television and air-conditioning and built an underground car park. Yet the ambience has remained, as has the priceless *mushrabia* work, Moorish vaulting and irreplaceable furniture. The marble pool is long gone and there is now a large modern one in which you can see the reflection of the Great Pyramid as well as swim in its shadow. There is also a golf course. A shuttle service to Cairo operates for guests. 5-star

Ramada Renaissance, Gîza Pyramids area (tel: 02 3877700).

With 520 rooms including 31 split-level suites. 24-hour room service. TV in all rooms, health club, four restaurants, shopping arcade and landscaped swimming pool. 5-star

Shopping

Off to the left on your way out to the Pyramids from Cairo is **Horrenaya** village. Here a building was set up some years ago to give work to youngsters with no carpet-making experience. The building is on the Saqqâra Road some 2 miles (3.5km) south from the Pyramids Road. The workers were shown how to weave and allowed to design what they wished as long as it made a picture. Many turned out to be gifted, and fresh young talent continues to join the enterprise. Today Horrenaya rugs have become famous and have been exhibited in Europe. Some are small enough for a telephone table and are a good buy to bring home.

HELIOPOLIS

About 6 miles (10km) from Cairo's centre is the suburb of **Heliopolis**, built in the early part of this century as a luxurious residential area for the capital's wealthy citizens. Of interest to the visitor is the granite **Obelisk of Heliopolis**. It was set up by Senusert I in the second millennium BC with a companion obelisk, both capped with copper and 66 feet (20m) high. They stood before one of the great temples in the rich city of On – Bible-readers will remember that Joseph married a daughter of Potiphar, a priest of On. Parts of the city (which the Greeks renamed Heliopolis) were razed to the ground by the fury of the Persian conqueror Cambyses, and by 24 BC, according to the Greek historian Strabo, it was in ruins. Arab writers claim that many statues were still *in situ* at the end of the 12th century. The fabled phoenix was supposed to be reborn there every 500 years. Whatever the truth, all that remains of the ancient city now is the obelisk, the oldest in Egypt.

Not far away from the obelisk is an old sycamore tree known as the 'Virgin's Tree'. It was planted in 1672 using a shoot from another gnarled sycamore, which had been an object of pilgrimage during the 14th century. It was believed that beneath its shade Mary had rested with the Christ Child after crossing the desert. Empress Eugénie, wife of Napoleon III of France, expressed a wish to see the tree when she was in Egypt, and the ruler of the country, Khedive Ismail, presented it to her! Wisely she left it where it was.

Coming right up to date, a new convention centre is being built in Heliopolis with the aid of the Chinese. With an auditorium to seat 2,500, a total capacity of 5,000 and its own hotel it will be probably the largest such centre in the Mediterranean. Several big international meetings have convened in Cairo and, as it is becoming increasingly accessible and is reasonably priced due to the favourable rate of exchange, it seems likely that many more visitors will be combining business with pleasure in Egypt.

EXCURSIONS FROM CAIRO – MEMPHIS AND SAQQÂRA

Accommodation

Baron Heliopolis, off Oruba Street (tel: 02 29124687). Overlooking the Imperial Baron Emplain Palace in Heliopolis, 10 minutes from the airport and close to the International Fair and Exhibition centre. 4-star

El Salaam, 61 Shari Abdul Hamid Badawy (tel: 02 2452155). The hotel is conveniently situated near the airport. The lobby is decorated in Georgian Wedgwood style and the hotel has its own swimming pool and gardens. There is a sporting club near by. 5-star

Le Meridien, 51 Oruba Street (tel: 02 2905055). Conveniently located in the district of Heliopolis, this hotel has a Venetian restaurant, plus disco, swimming pool, shopping arcade and business centre. 5-star

Novotel Cairo Airport, situated beside the airport. 4-star

MEMPHIS AND SAQQÂRA

The most important city of Egypt from the 3rd millennium BC to the coming of the Greeks, Memphis itself has largely vanished. Its former glory is now apparent only in its 'city of the dead', the necropolis, or cemetery, of Saqqâra.

◆
MEMPHIS RUINS

The site lies between Saqqâra and the Nile, some 10 miles (16km) from Cairo. Nothing remains today except a huge statue of Ramses II and an alabaster sphinx. Another statue of Ramses was there, but in recent years it was removed and placed in front of Cairo's main railway station. Its companion still lies at Memphis surrounded by a gallery which enables it to be viewed and photographed from

Statue of Ramses II, Memphis

all angles. Near by is the 18th-century BC alabaster sphinx, left exactly over the place from which it was excavated. It is surrounded by palm-lined pathways.

◆◆
PYRAMID OF UNAS
Saqqâra
This pyramid, belonging to the last king of the Vth Dynasty (about 2375–2345 BC), might almost be a craggy hill from its outside appearance. You enter through a large opening at the base and are surprised to find yourself in tidy passages leading to various chambers which look as if their wall illustrations had been painted yesterday. It was opened up in 1881 at the expense of Thomas Cook the travel agent. Its original height was 62 feet (18m) and at the base it measured 220 feet (67m). There had been various attempts to break into the pyramid centuries ago and one of the excavators, Ahmed the Carpenter, left his name inside in red paint. He is believed to be the same man who opened the Pyramid of Cheops at Gîza in AD 820.

◆◆◆
PYRAMID OF ZOSER
Saqqâra
Zoser was a pharaoh of the IIIrd Dynasty. His pyramid, the so-called Step Pyramid, is a pleasant place for a picnic lunch as well as a base for exploring the Saqqâra area. The pyramid is the only one of its kind and predates those at Gîza. It is considered to represent a staircase to heaven as it goes upwards in six steps on four

sides to its peak. It was built by Imhotep, an architect, statesman and physician of exceptional skill, whose tomb is thought to be close by but has not yet been found. He was deified in the 6th century BC.

◆◆
THE SERAPEUM
Saqqâra
This is another of the tombs in the necropolis of Saqqâra. From a passage over 100 yards (92m) long hewn in the rock a number of burial chambers

The Step Pyramid of Zoser at Saqqâra is the earliest pyramid in Egypt

lead off. Here mummified sacred bulls were placed in sarcophagi. Known as Apis bulls, they were worshipped up to the Graeco-Roman period.
The tomb was built by order of Ramses III, though the exact date is not known. Graveyards for other mummified creatures – baboons and ibises – have also been found near by.

◆◆◆
TOMB OF TI
Saqqâra
This Vth Dynasty tomb is one of the most beautiful at Saqqâra. The life of the handsome nobleman Ti is depicted in painted bas-relief. He obviously loved outdoor pursuits; he is shown hunting and fishing in lovely countryside and there is an appealing scene showing a baby hippopotamus trying to climb on to its mother's back. In another scene, Ti and his wife Neferhotpes watch animals being led to a temple for sacrifice, antelopes held by their horns, cattle in ceremonial collars.

THE FAIYÛM OASIS

You can reach the Faiyûm, an area of some 500 square miles (1,300sq km), by bus or car from Cairo, leaving along the Pyramids Road and bearing right at Mena House Oberoi hotel. The tarmac stretches in an almost straight line for about 60 miles (95km) to the Faiyûm. On the outskirts of the oasis at Karanis there is a little museum, a rest house and a shop where you can have a cooling drink or buy such things as fresh olives and honey.

◆
MUSEUM
The museum, which has some interesting exhibits, displays a small stone crocodile just inside the entrance. The Greeks called the capital city of the Faiyûm Crocodilopolis, for it was sacred to the crocodile god Sobek who was worshipped there. Four mummies are in a wonderful state of preservation and in a glass cabinet there are some tiny

figures of Bast, the cat-headed goddess. Some examples of the famous Faiyûm Portraits can be seen. Dating from Roman times, they are painted in a style called encaustic, by which the wax paint was burned in, and are amazingly lifelike. The best of them are of astonishing force.

◆
THE TOWN
The town of **El Faiyûm** has a population of over 140,000. In the centre, on a traffic island, stands an obelisk erected by the pharaoh Sesostris in the XIIth Dynasty. It is 40 feet (12m) high, made of granite and covered with pharaonic inscriptions. Otherwise there is not much of interest to tourists in the town itself. There are small shops and markets selling local produce. Leaving the town to the north you come, in about 10 miles (16km), to the shores of Birket (Lake) Qârûn. The lake is smooth and placid for the most part, spreading into the far distance where water and sky meet. There are fishing and watersports here, but bathing in the lake is unsafe because of bottom mud.

Accommodation
The 4-star **Auberge du Lac** (tel: 084 700002) on the shore of Birket Qârûn, was formerly the shooting lodge of King Farouk. Now a country club, it has been remodelled with every modern amenity including squash, tennis courts and riding stables yet it retains much of its lavish décor. The 3-star **Panorama** restaurant and hotel, set in a grove of trees and also on the lake shore (at

Desert Garden
Just beyond the museum the road cuts through the green of the oasis. The landscape on either side is flat like Holland and, like Holland in summer, it is lush with rich vegetable plots and canals.

Visitors to Egypt often notice that on menus the most luscious food is described as coming from the Faiyûm. Some of the finest turkeys, chickens and vegetables really do come from this garden in the desert. Rose growing is extensive for, from this flower is prepared the rose water so popular throughout the Middle East.

The oasis is also a fruit-growing area and back in pharaonic times was regarded as the orchard of Egypt. There is an impressive range of almond, apricot, orange, lemon, pomegranate, fig and olive groves. Tall acacias, tamarisks and eucalyptus trees cast dappled shadows on the grass. If you stop your car and listen you can hear the faint music of hundreds of water-wheels. The sugar cane grows high and sometimes lurking among the purple stalks you may glimpse a feral cat. The white egret too is found everywhere in the Faiyûm, following the plough or wading in the paddy-fields.

Shaksheik), and the 2-star **El Syllin** in the village of that name are two other places where you can stay in reasonable comfort. El Syllin itself, some 5 miles (8km) from El Faiyûm, is known for its mineral water springs. It has a small, pretty park with a restaurant and chalets.

ALEXANDRIA AND THE MEDITERRANEAN COAST

Between Cairo and the north coast lies the area generally referred to simply as 'the Delta', that area of alluvial soil deposited by the arms of the Nile, forming a triangle enclosed by Alexandria, Port Said and Cairo. It is a large area and, after Cairo itself, the most densely populated one. Much of it is agricultural, there is some industry and it does not receive much attention from tourism. The chief towns are Tanta, Zagazig and Damanhûr, while Damietta (Dumyat) and Rosetta (Rashid) are on the coast at the two main outlets to the Mediterranean. The famous Rosetta Stone, now in the British Museum, was found at Rosetta. This proved to be the key which enabled Champollion to decipher the Egyptian hieroglyphics.

ALEXANDRIA

The largest port in Egypt as well as a holiday resort, Alexandria is situated on the west shoulder of the Nile Delta. If you visit it by car from Cairo it is a journey of about 140 miles (225km) along what is called the agricultural road through the Delta via Benha, Tanta and Damanhûr. Part of it is a four-lane highway divided by shrubs and greenery down the centre and edged with canals which are often wide enough for *feluccas*. There are one or two cafés at which to stop on the way. You can also drive 155 miles (250km) along the desert road, which is the bus route.

The train journey from Cairo is another alternative. Frequent diesel services make the journey in less than three hours.
Should you arrive by air from Cairo you will see the city from another angle and land at a small airport surrounded by formal gardens. Alexandrian taxis are orange and black. One of these may take you through the city to your hotel. The route is attractive, passing by Nuzha Gardens with its zoo and then through the university quarter with its various faculties. Shari el Gaish runs along the seafront to the harbours. The western harbour is for commercial shipping, the eastern one concentrates on fishing and yachting.

History
In Alexander the Great's time (he conquered Egypt in 332 BC) the city lay on a narrow strip of land separating Lake Maryut from the Mediterranean. The two harbours were formed by a small island called Pharos which was joined to the land by a mole. On the northeast corner of Pharos a 600-foot (180m) lighthouse was built, one of the Seven Wonders of the Ancient World and the model from which the world's lighthouses were to be copied. By the 14th century successive earthquakes and long neglect had destroyed the city and all traces of the Pharos tower vanished. Not only had its high brazier guided the ships into harbour but it had housed a large garrison in its 300 rooms. Silt widened the mole and the island of Pharos became a headland where

ALEXANDRIA

Pompey's Pillar with its companion sphinx is an Alexandrian landmark

Egypt's dynamic ruler, Mohammed Ali was, from 1834 to 1845, to build his favourite palace, Ras el Tin (see below), which commands the entrance to the western harbour. Alexandria was a great trading centre under the Ptolemies (a Greek dynasty whose last ruler was Cleopatra) with a mixed population of Egyptians, Jews and Greeks, and continued to be so under the Romans. Rhacotis was the Egyptian quarter where the Serapeum stood, a long since vanished temple, dedicated to the worship of Serapis, a cult introduced by Ptolemy I. It was situated on the hill on which stands **Pompey's Pillar** which is now almost the sole relic of ancient Alexandria. It is made of red granite from Aswân and its height, including pedestal and Corinthian capital, is 98 feet (30m). Two sphinxes are at the base of the pillar, which was erected in the 3rd century AD by the Roman Prefect in honour of the Emperor Diocletian. The royal palaces were at the east end of the city together with the famous Alexandrian library, with its wealth of ancient literature. The world owes much to Alexandrian scholars: Euclid, the geometrician; Hipparchus the astronomer; Ptolemy and Eratosthenes, the geographers; and Archimedes, the Greek mathematician. His method of raising water using a tube formed into a screw round a cylinder is still used in Egypt today.

Antony handed some 200,000 manuscripts over to Cleopatra and these became the foundation of a second library, but both were destroyed by Christian mobs in the fourth century AD. The name of Alexandria is inextricably associated with that of Cleopatra for it was there that she enchanted Julius Caesar. Later Antony spent several years with her in Alexandria. On the site now known as Saad Zaghloul Square she built a temple for Antony, but it was left unfinished at their deaths, and its embellishment was left to their conqueror Octavian (Caesar Augustus), who adorned it with two obelisks brought from Heliopolis, where they had been made during the reign of Tuthmosis III. One of these obelisks is now on the Thames Embankment in London, where it is known as Cleopatra's Needle, the other is in New York's Central Park.

The City Today

Modern Alexandria is a planned city. Much of it was built with profit made from Alexandria's monopoly of the cotton trade when the American Civil War caused a worldwide cotton shortage in the 1860s. It is a mixture of past and present. Take the tram to get the feel of the place. It halts at such evocative places as Cleopatra,

Camp Caesar, Stanley Bay, Glimonopoulo, terminating at Victoria.

Walk along the corniche and you may still catch snatches of Greek, Italian, French, English or Armenian amid the native tongue. The variety of restaurants also reflects the varied cultures of this once cosmopolitan city – Greek tavernas and Italian trattorias, French pâtisseries and very English tea rooms which serve clotted cream in the afternoons. In the centre of the city is Liberation Square with, on its north side, the Anglican St Mark's Church.

Christianity in Egypt spread from Alexandria where St Mark first preached the gospel, and he was subsequently martyred there. Alexandria's winding corniche with its string of white hotels is treeless and the focal point is Saad Zaghloul Square, approached along wide avenues edged with palm trees and flower beds. A statue of Saad Zaghloul, the statesman who negotiated with Britain for the independence of Egypt after World War I, is surrounded by lawns and flower troughs. There are benches on the corniche where you can sit and enjoy a view of the turquoise sea a few yards away. Zaghloul is posed in a standing position with, like many statues of Ramses II, one foot in front of the other, as if he was about to stride into the Mediterranean. A jauntily placed fez protects his head from the sun. From here there is a lovely view of the bay extending some 6 miles (10km) in a sweeping curve.

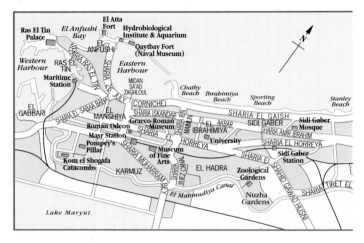

What to See in Alexandria

◆◆
CATACOMBS OF KOM
EL SHOGAFA
south of Pompey's Pillar
The catacombs date from the
Roman period, around the 2nd
century AD. They were
discovered in 1900 by accident
when a donkey and cart
vanished from view down a
yawning hole which suddenly
opened.
There are three levels (though
the bottom one is now flooded),
reached by a spiral staircase and
you can visit various funerary
chambers. The decoration is a
mixture of Graeco-Roman and
Egyptian styles, the latter, for
instance, in the form of a
representation of the wings of
Horus, and there are statues of a
woman and a man in pharaonic
costume. There is also a statue of
Anubis with the usual jackal
head, but the god is dressed as a
Roman soldier.

◆◆
GRAECO-ROMAN MUSEUM
off Horreya Avenue
Here you can see a collection of
5th-century stucco paintings of
saints and coloured geometrical
designs which come from
monasteries to the west of
Alexandria. There are also
textiles woven from wool and flax
with animal and plant designs,
while others have scenes from
Greek mythology. In the same
hall there is an alabaster statue
representing the Good Shepherd
with a lamb across his shoulders
and two smaller lambs sitting at
his feet. This museum has a maze
of bright rooms housing exhibits
from different periods of the
city's history: the beautifully
preserved statue of the Apis bull
excavated from ruins near
Pompey's Pillar, imposing
figures of gods and Roman
rulers, fine golden jewellery and
an incredible collection of coins.
Only a few of the latter are on
exhibition but the museum

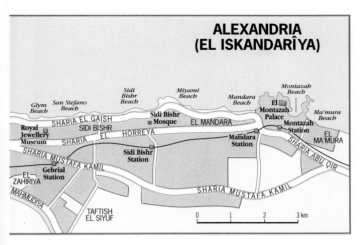

ALEXANDRIA (EL ISKANDARÎYA)

possesses some 50,000. Most fascinating of all perhaps is a beautiful collection of genuine Tanagra figurines of the 4th century BC. These tiny terracotta statuettes, from Alexandria's ancient tombs, are of inestimable value, and they are very well displayed on glass shelves. They still retain some of their original colouring of blue, green and pink, and each statuette stands in a different posture.

A passage leads to a garden and you are once again conscious of the advantages of the dry, sunny Egyptian weather, for on display in the gardens are further exhibits – as safe out of doors as under cover. One comprises two large tombs of the 1st and 3rd centuries. There is a statue of Ramses II with his daughter, a bust of Antony as Osiris, and two granite sphinxes from Heliopolis. The garden is delightfully quiet save for the chirping of many birds – an ideal spot for a moment of repose.

◆
HYDROBIOLOGICAL INSTITUTE AND AQUARIUM

Situated on El Anfushi bay, near Qaytbay Fort, the aquarium here contains a large variety of rare fish and marine species, including lion fish, flying fish, butterfly fish and others from the Nile and the Red Sea.

◆
QAYTBAY FORT (NAVAL MUSEUM)

To the north of the city where the famous Pharos lighthouse once stood, is Qaytbay Fort on the very tip of the eastern harbour. This medieval structure, built in the 15th century, looks like a Beau Geste fort with its turrets, embrasures and crenellated battlements. Some masonry from the Pharos was used in the building and can be seen. It is now the Naval Museum. On the first floor there are paintings and dioramas of pharaonic boats and sea battles.

ALEXANDRIA

The Qaytbay Fort occupies the site of the ancient Pharos lighthouse

Succeeding halls and floors have other paintings and models of Egyptian boats and scenes of naval history up to the present.

◆
RAS EL TIN PALACE

Sightseeing is not difficult as Alexandria is laid out on the grid system used in many modern cities. A number 8 bus will take you to the palace of Ras el Tin (Cape of Figs), now used for government purposes and official entertainment. The palace was built by Mohammed Ali between 1834 and 1845. One of the larger palaces in Egypt, it is situated on the seafront at the western end of the city. It was in the Attendants Hall with its red plush chairs that, on 26 July 1952, King Farouk sat with the American Ambassador waiting for the last paper he was to sign

in Egypt – the instrument of abdication. The palace is not open to the public.

◆◆◆
THE ROMAN ODEON ✓

Excavations in the 1960s at Kom el Dikka in the centre of Alexandria disclosed a Graeco-Roman open-air theatre, the only one of its kind in Egypt, built probably towards the end of the 2nd century AD. It was discovered after levelling an artificial hill and dismantling an old fort. Excitement was intense as the archaeologists went deeper and gradually uncovered the ancient building. There are two entrances to the site, one from Shari Abdel Moneim, close to the main railway station and the other from Shari Safiya

Zaghloul. You walk along banks set with flowerbeds and edged with trees to gaze down at the stage. Twelve rows of white marble seating radiate upwards in a semi-circle.

ROYAL JEWELLERY MUSEUM
Al Ahmed Yehia Street
This museum houses a delightful collection of jewellery and ornaments formerly belonging to Mohammed Ali's family.

Accommodation
Al Salamlek, Muntazah Palace (tel: 03 860585). This was once a royal pavilion. Stands back from the sea in the grounds of the old palace. 4-star
Montazah Sheraton, Corniche el Nil, El Montazah (tel: 03 5480550). The hotel borders the Mutazah Palace park, it has 307 rooms. 5-star
Palestine Hotel, Muntazah Palace (tel: 03 5474033). This is a Helnon hotel, magnificently situated in the park of the Muntazah Palace, formerly the residence of King Farouk. The palace overlooks the sea and its long driveway passes up through a eucalyptus forest. The hotel is next door. 5-star
Pullman Cecil Hotel, 16 Saad Zaghloul Square (tel: 03 807055). A spacious hotel in the centre of the city on a bus route. Minibars and TV in rooms. Good food. 4-star
Windsor Hotel, 17 El Shuhada Street (tel: 03 808700). Close to the Cecil and on the corniche. The shops are near and there is a view of the harbour. Has a pavement café in front. 4-star

The Beaches
Alexandria is famous for its numerous sandy beaches. Going from east to west these are: Ma'mura, Muntazah, Mandara, Asafra, Miyami, Sidi Bishr, San Stefano, Glym, Stanley, Sidi Gaber, Sporting, Ibrahimiya and Chatby. All these stretch along the corniche. On the western boundaries of the city lie the suburbs of Agami and Hannoville. These are also renowned for their sandy beaches – though latterly some of these beaches have suffered from litter and pollution. You can hire boats, go fishing, play volleyball, swim or just laze. There are cafés and adjacent restaurants.

Shopping
The main city centre shopping area has branches of some of Cairo's largest stores but rather

---

Women in Egypt
The Egyptian attitude towards women may come as a surprise in a country well used to tourists. Local women do not, for instance, usually sunbathe on beaches in swimsuits and, if they brave the sea, may well do so fully dressed. Also, Egyptian women do not drink in bars or travel around with men who are not their husbands.
To minimise unwelcome attention, it is best for female tourists to avoid wearing revealing clothes, sitting alone in bars or cafés or going on *felucca* trips on their own. On buses sit in the section reserved for women or close to other women. A precautionary wedding ring can deter pestering, but if a problem persists, make a loud fuss and seek the nearest Tourist Police officer.

cheaper prices. Alexandria is the home of the best cotton in the world. Here you can buy linen, cotton jersey, voile, gaberdine and other cotton weaves in lovely designs, and also pure silk at less cost than in Europe or America. There are good antiques to be bought, and the best known antique shop, **Habashi**, is also in this area. There are also many shops where you can buy leather goods and order hand-made shoes which are too reasonable in price to resist.

WEST OF ALEXANDRIA

The Mediterranean coast of Egypt, relatively undiscovered by foreign tourists though its resorts are popular with native Egyptians, stretches west from Alexandria more than 300 miles (500km) to the Libyan frontier. It is best to hire a car for a journey west of Alexandria, rather than to rely on the train service. Memories of World War II are strong as you follow the north coast.

EL ALAMEIN

About 60 miles (100km) west of Alexandria lies El Alamein. The name seems prophetic, for in Arabic it means 'Two Flags'. Over 50 years ago German and Allied forces were locked in combat here. Today thousands of their servicemen lie enshrined beneath their flags and El Alamein is now a place of pilgrimage.

If you wish to visit the war cemeteries from Alexandria in a day, you need an early start. Once beyond the outskirts of the city you drive along an asphalt road shimmering in the sun which stretches, a thin black line, between extensive fig groves tended by bedouin, in turn giving way to desert. The lonely railway line to Mersa Matrûh is on your left.

To the right the fawn sand gradually merges into startlingly white dunes and beyond them you suddenly see the Mediterranean. In bright sunlight the sea is an unbelievable delphinium blue. If it is early summer, distant specks of yellow and green by the roadside resolve themselves into laburnum trees, heavy with blossom, close by the Alamein Rest House. Spiky cactus plants edge a little road off to the desert on the left, leading to a gateway and an arched white cloister. A plaque reads: 'Within this cloister are inscribed the names of soldiers and airmen of the British Commonwealth and Empire who died fighting on land or in the air where two continents meet and to whom the fortunes of war devised a known and honoured grave with their fellows who rest in the cemetery with their comrades in arms of the Royal Navy. They preserved for the West the link with the East and turned the tide of war.'

Through the central arch you can see a high cross, and between plots of green grass there are neat beds of flowers. Everything is quiet, the individual graves beautifully kept. Badges of the various regiments are carved on the tombstones. They have no names, but bear the words: 'Four soldiers of the 1939–1945 war – known unto God.'

British war cemetery at El Alamein, a moving reminder of World War II

The tombstones all look alike but the engravings are as individual as the men who rest beneath. The German cemetery is a few miles further on. Here the memorial is a large tower rather like a medieval castle. It is open to the sky and within its precincts are large alcoves, each with a mass grave. Beneath a huge sarcophagus in each alcove lie 500 soldiers of the renowned Afrika Korps. The Rommel memorial is in a white enclosure. Along the road still further west is the Italian cemetery, with a small white museum at the entrance containing charts, maps and weapons used during World War II. The memorial itself takes the form of a high cone with a vaulted ceiling. Half the wall is glass, the rest is inscribed with the names of the fallen. An altar with a statue of the Virgin Mary is usually covered with flowers. A staircase winds upwards to the ceiling with oblong openings. The wind comes in through them

with a sighing sound. It is a sad but beautiful place.

Because El Alamein is the narrowest point between the Qattâra Depression to the south (a vast basin of sand and salt marshes edged by sheer cliffs) and the sea, it was chosen by the Allies as the best place to give battle to the Axis powers and exclude them from the Delta. Today it is calm and peaceful and its blue waters across white sand are inviting for swimmers. Only the quiet cemeteries are a reminder of the conflict which once raged here.

◆
MERSA MATRÛH
Mersa Matrûh, 180 miles (290km) west of Alexandria, again brings back memories of the last war. In the headland across the harbour is Rommel's Grotto, an underground headquarters cut into the rock which has been turned into a small museum. Today Mersa

WEST OF ALEXANDRIA

Matrûh is a holiday resort popular with Egyptians, with an excellent beach sheltered from the sea by a chain of rocks. The town is a meeting place of many different peoples – including desert bedouin North African emigrants and Greeks. To wander through the streets past small shops and cafés, seeing unusual people and attractive local products for sale, is a pleasant relaxation.

SIDI ABD EL RAHMAN
Between El Alamein and Mersa Matrûh is the small exclusive seaside resort of Sidi Abd el Rahman. This area is well known for its dry air, crystal waters and white sandy beaches.

SIWA
Siwa oasis lies in the middle of the desert about 190 miles (306km) southwest of Mersa Matrûh. Some people still think of an oasis as a small spring in the midst of nowhere but in fact Siwa is 50 miles (80km) long by 5 miles (8km) wide and contains a sizeable township.
There are about 200 springs, some salt, some sweet, some hot, some cold. There is a large cultivated area with date palms and olive groves. Some of the springs are used for the treatment of various illnesses. The 5th-century BC Greek historian and traveller Herodotus relates that in the early morning some springs were warm and became colder as the day warmed up, while others reached their maximum temperature in the middle of the night.
The oasis has been known since

1100 BC and Alexander the Great visited its renowned temple of Amen in 331 BC, when its oracle confirmed his divinity. Siwa was formally annexed to Egypt in 1820.
The journey to Siwa is along a surfaced road. There is a daily bus service from Mersa Matrûh, or you can share a taxi. You will need a permit from the General Authority for the Promotion of Tourism at the Governorate Building in Mersa Matrûh. This is required to keep a check on travellers.
The bus journey from Matrûh takes about five hours; it makes a rest stop, but you should carry water with you anyway. It can be hazardous if you are caught in a sandstorm, so always travel in convoy. The oasis is well worth visiting.

Accommodation
In Mersa Matrûh 3-star hotels include the **Radi**, El Corniche Street, Old Minia (tel: 03 944828); and the **Beau Site**, El Shatee Street (tel: 03 9432066).
El Alamein in Sidi Abd el Rahman (tel: 03 4921228) is 4-star with 209 rooms and villas – the villas are self-contained with sunshades at the sea's edge. There are also private villas for rent. A tourist camp is run by the local council.

Minefields
If you see a fenced-off stretch of beach, keep your distance. Mines from World War II may still lurk under the Mediterranean sands. Similar mementoes remain round the Red Sea Coast and in inland Sinai.

The Suez Canal, one of the world's most vital passages for trade

THE SUEZ CANAL, THE RED SEA AND SINAI

◆◆◆
THE SUEZ CANAL

From the carvings on the walls of Karnak temple, it is known that a canal joining the Nile and the Red Sea existed during the reign of Seti I (about 1312–1290 BC). In 521 BC, the Persian king Darius reopened the canal from Cairo to Suez. A few centuries later, after the departure of the Romans, the canal had been allowed to silt up. It was intermittently reopened by the Arabs, but for strategic reasons they preferred it to remain unnavigable.

The Suez Canal's 100 miles (160km) flow through Lake Timsâh and the Great Bitter Lakes. Its width between the lakes in the early days was a mere 100 yards (90m). Today it has been widened beyond recognition to take the big ships which use it nowadays. Port Said (see below), built on the dredgings of the canal, became known as the Gateway to the East in Victorian times. It was a city of beach villas and green squares. In the days of the great ocean liners it was a mecca for passengers coming ashore for a few hours. There were famous shops like Simon Artz, and jewellery, leather goods, watches and other items were much cheaper than in Europe.

THE SUEZ CANAL

Much has changed along both sides of the canal since the last two World Wars and the bitter fighting of 1973. Then, ships were scuttled, mines were laid and it became impassable to shipping. Indeed 15 vessels of eight different nationalities were marooned in the Great Bitter Lakes. For months the famous waterway ceased to function. Then, as suddenly as the fighting had begun it ceased. On 5 June 1975 the canal was formally reopened by President Sadat, its waters having been cleared by the combined efforts of the Egyptians assisted by the navies of several other countries. Today shipping noses its way past the three canal townships as if nothing had happened.

What to See Around the Suez Canal

PORT SAID

Port Said has been rebuilt and its harbour and docks enlarged to cope with increased numbers of cruise and freight ships. Here passengers land to get expensive goods duty free. There are tree-lined squares, gardens, a small military museum and a new National Museum. There is a rail link between Port Said and Cairo. Egyptians themselves come from the capital to shop because, even though they pay duty when they leave the zone, they save money. Passengers can leave their ships here, arrange a tour within Egypt and rejoin their ship at Suez. There is transport of various kinds for sightseeing, visits to the canal townships, Cairo or even further afield.

Making the Canal

Napoleon dreamed of linking the Red Sea with the Mediterranean, and he made a few attempts to do so. But it took another Frenchman years later to make the dream become a reality – Ferdinand de Lesseps. De Lesseps had endless difficulties before achieving success but he had two major advantages: he won the Egyptian Khedive Mohammed Said over to his way of thinking, and the Empress Eugénie was his cousin. She was very intrigued with De Lesseps' idea of linking the two seas and awakened the interest of her husband Napoleon III.

At last, with the backing of an international commission representing various European countries, the work was begun in the 1850s and finished in 1869. At one time there were more than 20,000 workers. Several thousand camels brought drinking water for them from the Nile until finally a fresh water canal was constructed, known to this day as the Sweetwater Canal.

Once the amazing project was completed the Empress Eugénie was invited to come and declare the canal open.

For those who continue along the canal by ship, it is interesting to traverse Lake Timsâh where there are yachts and other ships anchored awaiting passage. Sometimes you can watch fishermen about to haul in a catch. Their fishing technique involves forming their boats into a circle, then lowering their nets over the sides and beating the water with sticks making a drumming noise which frightens the fish into the

Port Said, a consumer's paradise for duty-free goods, has some attractive buildings

nets. Along the shore stand lone fishermen, knee-deep in the water, whirling their handnets above their heads and, with a deft rotating movement, casting them into the water in perfect circles. Edged with small weights, the nets fall quickly to the bottom trapping any fish within the circle. These nets look small from a distance but are at least 10 feet (3m) in diameter, held by a long line attached to the centre.

◆
ISMAILIA (ISMÂ'ILÎYA)
Facing Lake Timsâh is the town of Ismailia. Named after the Khedive Ismail; it is the

headquarters of the Suez Canal Company where many of the administrative staff and pilots live. The office buildings are large and airy, the clubs and villas charming. Hidden from the roads by walled gardens they face on to jacaranda-lined streets. A small park has statues dug up from the canal during the excavations, which you can glimpse through bougainvillaea and other shrubs. A small pink marble museum backs on to the park, again full of curios from the canal. There are mummy cases, statues and hieroglyphic cut stones. Other cases contain head ornaments, bracelets of all sizes, large loop earrings, turquoise jewels, rings, anklets beaded with lapis lazuli and scarabs. When Ramses II caressed the tawny mane of his pet lion, perhaps one of the cornelian rings was on his forefinger and shone through the thick fur with the same lustre that it has today.

Villas give way to blocks of flats in the centre of the town. The Greek Orthodox Church, apricot in colour, overlooks a green square criss-crossed with paths and set with jacarandas and other flowering trees. Roads lead off the square, one being the main shopping street leading to another square and the town centre with its doctors, dentists, banks, main post office and some clubs. Near by is the railway station.

De Lesseps' villa has been turned into a small museum. There you can see his four-poster bed complete with mosquito net and his grey marble-topped washstand with its silver basin and brass ewer. Behind his simple desk faded pictures hang on the wall: family portraits, the opening of the canal in 1869, and representations of

The minaret of a mosque pierces the blue sky in charming Ismailia

small vessels in the waterway. One wonders what de Lesseps would have thought if he saw the giant ships of today, such as tankers displacing a quarter of a million tons, gliding through his famous masterpiece.

If you drive from Ismailia to Suez the road not only follows the canal but is full of interest. Beyond Nifisha Lagoon, on the right, look out for a war memorial on a hill overlooking the canal. It consists of two great granite pillars, the deep cleft between them symbolic of the canal. Two vigorous figures stand at the base staring out beyond the waterway and over the wastes of the Sinai. The monument is in memory of the canal defenders of World War I.

You soon come to the Great Bitter Lakes, much larger than Timsâh, with the town of Fâyid. Small bungalows have been built along the shore and there is sailing and swimming.

Driving along the remaining 30 miles (50km) to Suez you watch the canal gradually change colour, like a chameleon, from light blue to lime green.

◆
SUEZ

Round a sweeping semicircle in the road the Ataqa hills behind Suez appear. They are as devoid of greenery as those at Fâyid, but due to their rock formation are drenched in reddish colours from russet to pink, and it is from them that the Red Sea gets its name. They merge into the blue sky like a sunset.

The local people who are not shopkeepers or merchants work on the docks or at the large oil refineries on the outskirts. The harbour is crowded with ships flying the flags of all nations and it is interesting to watch tourists come ashore. Customs and passports are checked on board so no one is kept waiting. Passengers disembark into launches in the bay which bring them ashore, where there is a tourist office on the road from the jetty.

Twice a day there are express trains between Suez and Cairo with restaurants and air-conditioning. The journey takes about three hours. There are also air-conditioned coaches covering the same journey. A new shopping area with blocks of flats and other buildings has appeared beyond the *souks* and narrow lanes.

Port Taufiq is a mile or so further south on the opposite side of the canal. It has been practically rebuilt since the reopening of the canal and is again a pleasant residential area. Thirty four miles (55km) south of Suez is Ain Sukhna, noted for its beautiful beach and hot sulphur springs.

A few miles north of Suez a new road tunnel has been dug beneath the canal so that it is now possible to drive into the Sinai without using a ferry. This has opened up the whole peninsula to both tourism and commercial traffic.

Accommodation

There are two 3-star hotels at Port Taufiq. The older **Summer Palace** (tel: 062 224475) has been renovated and the newer **Red Sea** hotel (tel: 062 223334) has 81 rooms.

THE RED SEA

HURGHADA

One of the best known places on the Red Sea, Hurghada is some 250 miles (400km) south of Suez. There are daily flights from Cairo which take an hour and also a daily bus service. It is both a summer and winter resort and the starting point for deep sea fishing expeditions. Barracuda, sailfish, swordfish and tuna can be caught. There is snorkelling, windsurfing, scuba diving, picnics, glass-bottomed boat trips and other sports to be enjoyed. Local entrepreneurs will even make an underwater video of you in action and you can buy the tape to bring home. All necessary equipment can be hired, as can boats for day or overnight trips.

Hurghada has grown into a town of great interest and it is as pleasant to stroll through its streets as to walk along the sandy shore. The wide streets are lined with frontless shops where you can buy anything from fruit and vegetables to sea shells and enjoy souvenir hunting. The *souks* are inviting and there is a new aquarium in the town centre. Near the shore there is a new mosque and further along there are private beach bungalows.

Further along the coast there are several smaller places with similar sports facilities such as Safâga, Quseir, Marsa Alam and Berenice.

Accommodation

In the bay of Abu Menka is the 4-star **Hurghada Sheraton** hotel,

circular in shape (tel: 62 440785). Its shops and some of its 125 rooms face into a charming atrium with trees, shrubs and flower-beds.

Two miles (3km) along the beach is **Magawish Resort Village**, 4-star (tel: 62 440759), run by Misr Travel. There are some 300 chalets and 14 VIP suites with a central restaurant, snack bars and lounges. The diving centre has a decompression chamber. The coral reefs here are particularly beautiful. The site was well chosen, for the sea here is free of currents and undertows.

SINAI

This large triangular desert area lies between the Mediterranean coast in the north, Israel in the east, the Gulf of Aqaba in the southeast, the Gulf of Suez in the southwest and the Suez Canal. It was the scene of intense fighting in past years but has now opened up for tourism.
It was to the Sinai Peninsula that the ancient Egyptians went for their gold, copper and turquoise. It was on one of these mountains that Moses is

In the wilderness of Sinai

said to have received the Ten Commandments, and through the Sinai that the Virgin Mary fled with the infant Jesus.
Sinai is accessible by air, car and ferry. Good roads connect all the towns and resorts here.

What to See in Sinai

◆
EL ARÎSH
The capital of the North Sinai region, this popular resort lies towards the Israeli border. Civilisation in these parts dates from pharaonic days up to the Islamic conquest of Egypt. Now it is famed for its palm-shaded beaches and olive plantations. There is an Environmental Tourist exhibition with life-size bedouin scenes. An assortment of fabrics and basketwork is on sale. There is also a village bazaar and a museum. Erected over the remains of an ancient pharaonic site is a castle built by a Turkish sultan. Air Sinai has regular flights to El Arîsh from Cairo and there is a coach service from there taking seven hours.

◆◆◆
SAINT CATHERINE'S MONASTERY (DEIR SANT KATERIN) ✓

Sinai was a place of refuge for the early Christians from their Roman persecutors. There they found isolation in a place suitable for the contemplative life. Crusading knights were permitted to go there by order of Saladin who, despite the fervour with which he waged war, was tolerant towards his opponents' beliefs.

St Catherine's Monastery sits dramatically among the mountains of Sinai

The monastery was built by command of the Emperor Justinian in about AD 520. It was intended as a fortress-monastery, but when it was completed, the Emperor discovered that it was militarily unsound – missiles could be thrown from the towering mountain above it – and the architect and others responsible were executed. Save for this stern measure, no violence has ever been connected with Saint Catherine's. Up to the present day the monastery has never been attacked and the monks have lived there through the centuries in peace. The wells near by have never dried up and a small green valley alongside has continued to thrive. Napoleon called Egypt 'the most important country in the world'. His imagination was fired by their Egyptian, biblical and pharaonic antiquities and his personal retinue included artists, historians and archaeologists. He was particularly interested in Saint Catherine's. An expedition was arranged for two of his archaeologists to visit the place. When they reached the monastery the friendly monks were only too ready to show their holy treasures, among them a casket containing the bones of Saint Catherine, priceless illuminated manuscripts, the well of Jethro where Moses met Zipporah, and a small chapel within the precincts on the site of Moses' burning bush. Here candles had been burning for more than 1,300 years. The only disquieting news that the archaeologists brought back to Cairo was that recent floods, exceptional in the desert, had swept down the mountainside to the ramparts and undermined the eastern wall. Blocks of granite similar to those used by Justinian were sent with masons from Cairo to repair the damage. An interesting feature is the mosque which was built in AD 1106 within the perimeter during the Fatimid period in Egypt. It stands as a symbol of the mutual toleration between Christianity and Islam. The 6th-century mosaic within the dome of the church is one of the finest examples of Byzantine art to be seen anywhere.

The library is remarkable. The Greek manuscripts alone number 2,250. There are, in addition, 600 in Arabic and several hundred volumes in other languages. The library once held the famous 4th-century Greek manuscript, the *Codex Sinaiticus*, now in the British Library.

There are several ways to reach the monastery. From Cairo, Air Sinai has a twice-weekly service; the flights take about 45 minutes and land at a nearby airstrip. Air-conditioned buses leave Cairo every morning. In a valley below, a village has grown up where there is a restaurant and

about 130 chalets. Just outside the monastery is an ossuary where the bones of monks, unearthed from their graves after several years, can be seen by visitors.

Many international students and groups of young people visit Sinai and it is advisable for their scanty baggage to include training shoes and heavy jackets for, although the days are sunny and warm, the nights can be extremely cold. Behind the monastery soars Moses' Mountain, the Mount Sinai of the Bible, where Moses is said to have received the Ten Commandments. Many visitors are tempted to climb the steps which have been cut by the monks – there are 3,750 of them!

◆

SHARM EL SHEIKH

There are a number of popular tourist sites in southern Sinai facing the sea, notably Sharm el Sheikh at the southern tip, which is acclaimed for its underwater activities; several coral reefs are only a few feet from the shore. It has a fully equipped diving club, and there are chalets and a boat with cabins which tours for several days at a time offering diving in different places. Deep-sea fishing, windsurfing, water-skiing and yachting are available, and there is an international airfield.

Accommodation

Sharm el Sheikh has the **Fayrouz Village** and **Ghazala Village**, plus the **Marina Sharon Hotel**, which all cater for watersports and offer bungalow accommodation. There are also bungalows at **Cliff Top Hotel**.

NILE CRUISING ✓

No other river in the world has so many interesting features or enjoys so romantic a reputation as the Nile. Along this highway 30 years ago, only a handful of pleasure steamers merged with the river traffic. Today well over 200 floating hotels, some carrying as many as 300 passengers, ply between Cairo and Aswân.

Among the reasons for the success of this type of holiday are good weather, the proximity of the antiquities to the river (which, after all, brought them into existence) and the calm water which eliminates motion sickness. A major consideration is that, instead of constant packing and unpacking and transfer to plane, train or bus, your accommodation accompanies you, as do the guides who brief you before you go ashore for the day's sightseeing.

Five-star, 4-star and 3-star cruises are available as package deals. They all visit the same main sites, but the accommodation, food and leisure facilities on offer range from deluxe to tourist according to the cruise grade. Ships are operated by travel organisations such as Swan Hellenic, Bales and Abercrombie and Kent, and also by hotel chains such as Hilton, Sheraton and Oberoi. The high season is between November and April – the heat during the summer months can reduce the pleasure of sightseeing.

The passing panorama as you cruise along is fascinating and, after an expedition ashore, it is

A Nile cruise is a popular and relaxing way of visiting the ancient sites

pleasant to know that your next meal awaits your return in an air-conditioned dining room and, should you be thirsty, a well-stocked bar is always open. The full Cairo–Aswân trip takes 10 to 12 days, four days being the minimum for the more commonly travelled Luxor–Aswân section. Most people fly to and from the ships but it can be done by a comfortable train journey as well.

The use of the terms Upper and Lower Egypt, upstream and downstream and north and south can be rather confusing at first. The Nile flows from south to north so Luxor and Aswân are upstream from Cairo. It is, of course, possible to do your

small statues holding even tinier ones of Horus on their knees. One, with a bared breast suckling a baby Horus, appears to wink at you.

BENI HASAN
After the modernity of El Minya, Beni Hasan, 11 miles (18km) south, is a completely different experience. Here you moor alongside a sandy bank where a line of donkeys awaits your arrival, each held by a man who helps you to mount. If you prefer to walk rather than ride you can easily keep up with the column along a flattish sandy trail. After about half an hour you come to the base of a mountain. Here you dismount and begin to climb some 200 steps. As they are divided into short flights with flat ground in between it is not too arduous, but it may be a strain for the elderly if it is hot, and there are no handrails.

At the summit you are confronted by a long row of 39 rock tombs. Only a few are open to the public, and of those to the north numbers 2 and 17 are the most commonly visited. The tombs are famous for the light they throw on the customs and manners of everyday life in ancient Egypt through their wonderful frescoes. From the ridge you get an excellent view downward across the Nile valley and can appreciate why this magnificent site was chosen as a final resting place for the powerful nobles of the region in the 2nd millennium BC. Most of the tombs which are open are now illuminated by fluorescent lighting powered by portable generators so that you

whole or part cruise in either direction, and the majority of tourists only do the section from Aswân to Luxor.

What to See Along the Nile

EL MINYA
The first place at which you can go ashore after leaving Cairo is El Minya, 150 miles (245km) south and well known for its university. The small town of **Mallawi**, not far away, is also worth a visit if possible, because of its small museum. In one room mummies are displayed using mirrors so that you can see all round the sarcophagi. Several of them have large eyes painted on their sides, making it seem as if the mummy is watching you. One cabinet contains wigs with elaborate hairstyles. There are

can see the interior decoration easily. Porticoes lead in through fluted pillars sometimes called proto-Doric because of their resemblance to Greek Doric, but which were, however, a type designed many centuries before they were used in Greece. The columns, many damaged and some missing, divide each tomb into aisles and there is often a niche in the far wall for the statue of a god or goddess. The most interesting feature of these tombs is the frescoes. These are painted line upon line over the whole wall, almost like the pages of a book, and they convey a vast amount of information.

Tomb 2 is that of **Ameni**, governor of the 16th nome (administrative district) in Egypt during the reign of Usertsen I during the XIIth Dynasty around 1900 BC. He was hereditary prince of the district and held the office of priest to various gods and goddesses. Pictures show the working of flint and metal; the making of beer, bows, pottery and stone vessels; the methods of ploughing; treading of corn; reaping; wine making; the manufacture of rope; the netting of fish and birds; and athletics including wrestling. The latter scene is famous and is thought to be one of the earliest surviving pictures of this sport. Many wrestlers of today have come to Beni Hasan to see this ancient representation of the sport. Time passes quickly at Beni Hasan and on your way down the flights of steps you will see your donkeys waiting patiently below to return you to your floating hotel.

TELL EL AMÂRNA

Some.40 miles (65km) south of Minya is Tell el Amârna, a collection of ruins and rock tombs of the 14th century BC. A few of these are open to visitors. Immense areas have been excavated and have revealed the short-lived capital city of the pharaoh Akhenaten, who broke away from the religious traditions of his ancestors, adopting a monotheistic sun-worship, and also broke away from the long-established capital, Thebes. He founded Amârna, known then as Akhet-Aten (the Horizon of the Sun). You can see a boundary stele in the cliffs to the north. On it is the famous mural, so often reproduced in books, showing Akhenaten and Queen Nefertiti accompanied by their little daughters, holding up their arms in veneration to the sun. An inscription on the mural commemorates the founding of the city.

One of the daughters was to marry Tutankhamun, and when he became pharaoh in 1346 BC they returned to Thebes and the old gods and goddesses. Tell el Amârna became a ghost capital and vanished until excavation again brought it to light.

ASYÛT

Asyût, 236 miles (380km) from Cairo, has a tree-lined corniche where passengers go ashore. It is the capital of the province of the same name and, incidentally, the birthplace of President Mubarak of Egypt. Its barrage forms part of the system for regulating the level of the Nile. The city lies back from the river near the foot of a mountain on which is a convent of the Virgin Mary. Asyût's greatest pride is its university. The buildings are ringed with lawns and flower-beds. The agricultural faculty has a veterinary department where animals are housed under ideal conditions, and a fish hatchery.

Once through the barrage, the boat glides between palm-lined banks, yellow cliffs, little villages and narrow fields. The onlooker is often struck by the constant movement of the people and animals. Men busily till the sloping terraces and fields, women herd flocks of sheep, by leading rather than driving them. Egyptian sheep are attractive except for their fat tails. As the camel stores water in its extra

Part of the beautiful decoration in the temple of Seti I, Abydos

stomach, so these sheep store food in their tails. At market, sheep's tail fat is the cheapest part of the carcass. The buffalo is always in evidence along the Nile for he helps the *fellah* (farmer) wherever there is arable land and turns the water-wheels.

◆◆◆
ABYDOS
The **Temple of Abydos**, built by Seti I around 1300 BC, lies some 6 miles (10km) from El Balyana, a riverside town where you dock and are taken by car or bus beyond the town limits and farms, until the greenery yields to the desert and you come to the temple.

It is one of the most atmospheric sites, famous as the birthplace of Menes, who united Upper and Lower Egypt in the 4th millennium BC, and reputed burial place of Osiris, the resurrected god who was judge

of the dead. The royal tombs of Egypt's Ist and IInd Dynasties are here, for people of importance wished to be laid at rest near the god. As a result, the graves reach to the outer walls, in complete contrast to the tombs of the later pharaohs, who wished no one to discover their final resting places in the Valley of the Kings.

The temple walls are covered with bas-reliefs and hieroglyphics and, although they seem confusing at first, you soon learn to understand what some of them mean. The decorations are considered to be the peak of perfection in the art of relief carving, and Seti I gave his talented artists every facility and encouragement. The reliefs are unlike the sculptures of the reign of Ramses II, the great warrior who followed Seti I and who insisted on incisive, definite lines emphasising power and determination. Fate has been kind to Seti's part of the temple, for much of the beautiful colouring remains. There is a carving showing the pharaoh offering an image to Osiris. Another shows him proffering wine to Horus.

In a roofless antechamber Seti is shown teaching his son how to lasso a wild bull. On a wall in a long gallery you can see the famous tablet of Abydos, that amazing catalogue of the 76 dynastic kings of ancient Egypt. Egyptologists have found this genealogical tree most helpful and from it know that many pharaonic tombs have not yet been uncovered. Although the tablet is not a comprehensive list and does not give the names of the pharaohs before the unification of Upper and Lower Egypt, it has proved to be a unique key to the past.

> **Security at Abydos and Dendera**
> Before travelling to Abydos and Dendera you should check the security situation with your government or the local authorities, as there have been terrorist incidents in recent years.

◆◆◆
DENDERA

Napoleon thought the temple of Hathor here the most beautiful in Egypt but, being the last one before reaching Luxor, it is sometimes missed. Built in the Graeco-Roman period, it stands about 3 miles (5km) out of the town, its pylon pierced by six columns with Hathor heads as capitals.

As you enter the hypostyle hall, you see the lintel overhead sculptured with the wings of Horus. The hall has a central aisle and three rows of pillars on each side. Instead of lotus flower or papyrus capitals, each of the 24 pillars is again topped with a Hathor head. Turquoise blue still adheres to the broad foreheads, though much of the other colouring has peeled. On the ceiling is the figure of the sky goddess Nut.

In the sanctuary, a fresco shows Hathor being offered incense by a young pharaoh. It is held out to the goddess on a carved hand at the end of a slender staff. Many temple drawings show incense being offered in this way,

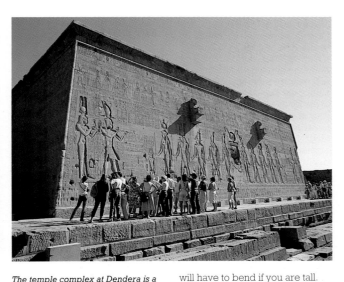

The temple complex at Dendera is a mixture of styles and periods

whereby the human was kept at a distance from the deity. From an antechamber you can ascend a staircase to a small shrine dedicated to Osiris called the Temple on the Roof. The ceiling is interesting in having in the centre a full-face carving. This is a replacement by the 19th-century Egyptian ruler Mohammed Ali, who had the original cut out and sent to Paris as a gift in 1821. It is now in the Louvre. The walls are covered with reliefs of a mummified pharaoh being brought back to life by the occult powers of the god of fertility. Down below again there is a series of crypts forming a long narrow passage beneath the floor. After descending a flight of steps, you will need a torch or the candle the guide will offer you. It is not very high and you will have to bend if you are tall. Here there are exquisite murals which have retained their colouring and are in excellent condition. You can see the god Horus with feathers that look real enough to touch and a delightful portrait of Cleopatra.

The temple walls inside and out are inscribed with the names of Roman emperors. One of the outer walls is very famous for it boasts a carving of Cleopatra and Caesarion, her son by Julius Caesar. Here, Cleopatra is depicted in profile so that one cannot see the fatal beauty which so captivated Caesar and Mark Antony. Nevertheless, it is one of the most photographed walls in Egypt.

◆◆◆
LUXOR
A growing tourist resort with ever more hotels, Luxor is Egypt's richest treasure-house of

ancient history. It is the site of the New Kingdom capital, Thebes. In the temples of Luxor and Karnak it has two of the world's most magnificent religious buildings and near by is the amazing necropolis known as the Valley of the Kings.

As you sail along the Nile towards Luxor, the columns of Luxor temple gradually appear on the skyline. When the boat docks beside the corniche it will be bow to stern with other passenger boats. Flights of steps lead upward between flower gardens to the main road. Across the road is Luxor temple. Certainly the temples of Luxor and Karnak merit numerous visits for it is impossible to appreciate their many wonders in a day. You not only see glorious shrines but sense the fantastic power of pharaohs whose absorbing passion in building, however catholic their tastes, was for sheer size and massiveness.

It is difficult to decide which is the more beautiful of the temples, but Karnak, 2 miles (3.5km) north of the Luxor temple, wins as far as size is concerned, for it is the most spacious monument of its kind in the world.

You quickly get the feel of Luxor, as its main street, called (of course) El Nil, is where you land from your ship. Beside Luxor temple is the Winter Palace hotel, a small shopping centre and a few cafés. There are more hotels further along El Nil. The main street is usually busy with buses and taxis and you can hire bicycles for sightseeing. The main transport

Ancient Thebes

Thebes was a mighty city which acted as a setting not only for the temples of Karnak and Luxor, but for the other great mortuary temples whose remains still lie upon the western plain near the Valley of the Kings and the Valley of the Queens.

Thebes was the capital of Egypt 3500 years ago and of a great empire reaching north into Syria. From ancient sources we learn that it had great wealth, for the revenues of 65 townships poured into its coffers. Built on a wide plain intersected by the Nile, Homer's 'hundred-gated' city stretched some 12 miles (20km) to mountains on the east and west.

Thebes was sacked by the Persian king Cambyses, in 525 BC. The burning of the beautiful city was so complete that it left only fragments of precious metals scattered among the statues and the shattered framework of the temples. The devastation was so great that Thebes was abandoned for ever, to be buried by sand and silt, the ruins left much as we see them today.

in Luxor, however, is by horse and carriage – the garry. This is a delightful way to get around if you are not in a hurry.

Museum

North of the ETAP hotel you will find an excellent small museum. Exhibits are well lit and there are even a few precious items from the Tutankhamun tomb. A new room contains well-preserved statues excavated at Luxor Temple in 1989.

Luxor Temple

The creator of Luxor temple, Amenhotep III (XVIIIth Dynasty, 15th century BC), was aptly called the Magnificent. During his reign of 35 years he lavished most of his gold not on war and conquest, but on sculpture and temples. Egypt was at the height of her imperial power and the city obelisks literally glittered with gold. The pharaoh spent much of his time studying architectural designs and decided Luxor temple should be on the east bank of the Nile. The town grew around it. He was responsible for the great court and the hall of columns, indeed the latter was the first project of its kind and measured 623 feet (190m) long by 181 feet (55m) wide. About 100 years later Ramses II added a mighty double-colonnaded courtyard. When you enter, you will see a small mosque perched incongruously above the ruins. Many years ago, before the temple was excavated, a village had grown up within its protecting colonnades as has happened with other temples. When mud buildings crumbled in the past, no one cleared away the rubbish, which acted as foundations for new houses. In

Part of the great Luxor temple

time the temple disappeared completely and during the 14th century a religious leader named Abu Hagag built a mosque high above the courtyard of Ramses II. Because Abu Hagag was descended from a saint the mosque was much revered. When the villagers were rehoused elsewhere while the temple was being excavated, no one would take responsibility for removing the mosque so it was left where it was. It has been renovated several times and is still used. You may even hear the call to prayer from its minaret, the ringing voice a link between past and present.

Before entering the temple you must look at the magnificent pylon. Scrolled across the façade is the history of the battle of Qadesh, the great victory Ramses won over the Hittites on the Orontes in 1300 BC. A colossus of the pharaoh, built from a single block, stands with its back to the pylon close to the entrance.

The approach to the temple's main court is along a colonnade of seven pairs of pillars, the famous hall of columns. They rise 42 feet (13m), topped with papyrus blossoms whose filaments flatten out at the summits to support the heavy blocks of the architrave. During the 4th century Christians turned part of the temple into a church and you will be shown pictures, though probably Roman, not Christian, painted over pharaonic reliefs.

In another part of the temple there are relief murals showing splendid processions. Most lively is a line of dancing girls about to

somersault; each is bent backwards as far as the knees of the girl behind her with such elasticity that you wonder why the supple figures do not swing upright again. Music is playing, for it is festival time when the pharaoh is happy in the knowledge that he is one with Amen-Ra, the patron god of Thebes. In May 1987 music of a different kind was heard, when the hall of columns acted as backdrop for performances of Verdi's *Aida* with the tenor Placido Domingo in the leading part.

The temple has been torn down in places, changed and rebuilt. In one court, for instance, Alexander the Great ordered that four columns should be removed and replaced with a square mass of masonry, which was then carved with frescoes. Over centuries, the temple gradually disappeared under sand and rubbish until little more than a few column capitals was visible on the ground surface. A hundred years of excavation have rectified this, and the work of Amenhotep III and Ramses II is now admired by thousands every year.

Karnak Temple ✓

Karnak is about 2 miles (3.5km) north of the temple of Luxor. These two miles were once filled with a huge complex of temples, chapels, sacred lakes and processional ways, of which the temple seen today, dedicated to Amen, was only the largest. The circumference of Karnak is over 2½ miles (4km). For a one-

Karnak temple: statue of Ramses II in the Great Court

day visit, you should study a plan of the temple.

The genius of Amenhotep III is again apparent in the architecture. Added to it were the riches bestowed on Karnak by Thothmes III, gleaned from 17 Asian invasions. Far Eastern plants bloomed in the formal gardens and were copied by artists who carved them in bas-relief, so that wildfowl gracefully fluttered amongst tropical flowers instead of the usual reeds. In the Great Court built by Ramses II there is the usual array of statues that one associates with this pharaoh, his wife Nefertari standing knee-high between his legs, the double crown of Upper and Lower Egypt on his head, holding the sceptre and flail, symbols of his kingly authority.

Beyond the court a forest of towering columns marks the famous Hypostyle Hall.

The sacred lake is artificial and was created during the reign of Thothmes III (about 1490 BC). On a high plinth crouches a huge granite scarab guarding the lake. During the migratory season it is covered with birds of all kinds. Probably wildfowl were netted here in pharaonic times, for cages of wild birds were one of the most impressive gifts to offer to the gods.

It is still possible to visit the temple in the traditional way, by garry, and this is especially pleasant in the evening when there is a *son et lumière* presentation. You leave your carriage at the entrance and walk along the illuminated avenue of ram sphinxes into the temple where, standing among the illuminated pillars, you can listen to the story of Karnak from the beginning. Even in November, the heat of the day still rises from the sand and stone at your feet so that you remain warm. Coloured lights brighten and dim, scenes come and go, voices change and music fills the air. You move with the audience further and further into the temple. Later the story leads you to an open-air theatre behind the sacred lake where you remain seated until the end of the performance. Finally the lights fade, the voices recede and the music dies away. Only the granite scarab on his plinth remains watchful. Gradually your eyes adjust to the darkness and you can make your way back to your carriage. If you cannot remember which is your garry, don't worry. Your driver will know you.

♦♦♦
NECROPOLIS OF THEBES ✓

Across the Nile from the great temple complex of Luxor and Karnak is a vast 'city of the dead'. In deep valleys on the western side of the river, the bodies of pharaohs and nobles of the 2nd millennium BC were buried with all the ritual necessary to ensure their survival in the afterlife. The famous Valley of the Kings is only one part of this whole great necropolis. Each pharaoh built a mortuary temple some distance from his actual tomb, where his *ka*, or spirit, could receive offerings to sustain him in the other world, and enjoy ceremonies in his honour.

Valley of the Kings

A guided tour of the tombs is recommended so that you see everything of interest with minimum effort. Over 60 pharaohs' tombs have been discovered, but only a small number can be visited. The largest and best tomb, that of Seti I, is closed at the moment, but other interesting tombs are described below.

Ramses VI – Tomb 9. The pharaoh was very old when he died and work had continued on his tomb for many years so there is much to see. The decoration illustrates the journey to the afterlife, giving the complete text of the Books of the Dead.

Ramses IV – Tomb 2. The patterns of bright colours against an overall background of white, and the excellent lighting, make this a particularly attractive tomb to visit. There is much Graeco-Roman and Coptic graffiti throughout. Early Christian hermits sometimes dwelt in pharaonic tombs, and here to the right of the entrance, they have painted two haloed saints with their arms raised in prayer. The huge pink granite sarcophagus is covered with texts and magical scenes, while the ceiling above is decorated with the sky goddess Nut.

Tutankhamun – Tomb 62.
Pharaohs' tombs were designed and started at the beginning of

their reigns. As Tutankhamun died while still a boy there had been no time to prepare for his journey to the other world. The descent to his tomb is down a short staircase leading to a beautifully painted chamber which still contains his sarcophagus. This is the only royal tomb to have come down to us intact. Its fabulous contents can be seen in the Cairo Museum of Egyptian Antiquities.

Colossi of Memnon
These two seated figures of Amenhotep III probably once flanked the pharaoh's mortuary

Surrounded by agricultural land sit the Colossi of Memnon

temple which has long disappeared. Gargantuan and impassive, hands on knees, they sit brooding over the flat plain towards the Nile, survivors of 3,000 years. Second in size only to the Sphinx, they tower over 60 feet (18m) above ground. The shoulders are 20 feet (6m) across, the forearms from elbow to fingertip 15 feet (4.5m) and the fingers over 4 feet (1.2m) long. Originally each was carved from one huge piece of stone. The right-hand figure was reputed to 'sing' at sunrise after it had fallen in an earthquake in 27 BC. The statue was repaired some 200 years after the earthquake and thereafter ceased to sing.

Deir El Bahri
The mortuary temple of Queen Hatshepsut, who ruled as pharaoh for 20 years from about 1490 BC is magnificently sited in the mountainside at Deir El Bahri, a short distance east of the Valley of the Kings. The temple was designed by the architect Senenmut, Hatshepsut's favourite, whose tomb is near by. The temple is built in three pillared terraces against a semicircular backdrop of barren mountain. Colonnades lead into great halls and chambers and there are wall reliefs depicting Hatshepsut's life and times. The temple has been reconstructed so that its original magnificence can be appreciated today.

Medinet Habu
This is the name by which the mortuary temple of Ramses III (about 1198–1167 BC) is known. The walls show details of the pharaoh's life, with scenes of him judging his enemies, lion hunting and fighting a naval battle.

Tombs of the Nobles
The tombs of the nobles are notable for their beautiful painted scenes of everyday life, lacking in the more solemn royal tombs, and should be visited if time allows. They are clustered round (and under) the village of Sheikh el Gurna.

Valley of the Queens
In the Valley of the Queens the tomb of Nefertari, wife of Ramses II, has recently been restored and opened, the queen depicted in charming and vividly coloured wall paintings. Access is restricted, however, to only 150 people a day, so get there early and be prepared to pay the hefty special entrance fee.

ESNA
Another 34 miles (55km) south of Luxor your ship arrives at Esna and ties up near an old pier. After a few minutes' walk along the river bank you will reach the town and are suddenly in busy streets. Towards the centre you come to some railings where you can look down some 30 feet (9m) into a large excavation where stands the small temple. It was built in the Ptolemaic period and later embellished with reliefs and inscriptions describing events and rituals of the Ptolemies and the Roman emperors to the 3rd century AD. These are of immense importance to archaeologists. The temple is dedicated to the ram-headed god Khnum. Twenty-four deeply engraved

columns surround a large hall, which is all that has been excavated. During the Christian era two chambers were built into the façade of the building, one as a library and the other as a vestry for the priests.

◆◆◆
EDFU
Continuing south another 30 miles (50km) upriver, about halfway between Luxor and Aswân, the boat reaches the town of Edfu and its magnificent Ptolemaic temple of Horus. It was started in 237 BC by Ptolemy II and finished in 57 BC, the late date probably accounting for the fine state of preservation – even some of the roofs are still intact. You enter via the Court of Offerings, the first section in the temple's layout. Every wall surface is carved with pictorial reliefs and hieroglyphic inscriptions giving a unique account of religious rituals of the time. The most complete

Carving: temple of Horus, Edfu

monument in Egypt of its date, it stands alone, well away from the town. A large statue of Horus, in the form of a falcon wearing the double crown of Egypt, stands guard on the left side of a doorway, his wings folded.

◆◆◆
KOM OMBO
This Ptolemaic temple is 30 miles (50km) north of Aswân just around a curve in the river. It is dedicated to two deities, Sobek the crocodile god and Haroeris, the hawk-headed god of the morning sun. Everything is duplicated to avoid any jealousy, so there are twin sanctuaries and offering tables. There are mummified crocodiles in a small chapel to the side of the temple.

◆◆◆
ASWÂN
Most Nile cruises are between Luxor and Aswân. The boats turn round at both places and take on a fresh load of passengers. Aswân is the southern limit of navigation for Nile cruises as above here there are cataracts and the two dams. Above the High Dam, which was built with Russian aid between 1960 and 1972 and is one of the largest dams in the world, lies Lake Nasser, 300 miles (500km) long, reaching south into the Sudan.

Once ashore in Aswân, you can drive through a pleasant maze of streets out beyond the town to see the Old Aswân Dam (finished in 1902) and look down at the sluices through which the water thunders. Far below in a wide expanse of swirling water there are tree-covered islets and great jagged rocks with moss adhering to their sides.

Botanic Island

You take a *felucca* to visit this small island, often referred to as Kitchener's Island for it was presented to Kitchener when he was Consul-General in Egypt just before World War I, and there he indulged his passion for flowers. He loved the island and ordered plants from India and the Middle and Far East. An enchanting place to visit, it is now kept as a botanical island, a perfect place to end a day's sightseeing. Your *felucca* will sail round the island and be waiting at the far end by the time you have wandered across.

Granite Quarries

Red granite was an important product of Aswân in pharaonic times. The great obelisks erected in temple complexes were cut here and transported down to the northern cities when the river was in flood. A visit to the granite quarries, just a quarter of an hour's drive from the town by a route passing the Arab cemeteries, impresses the observer with the technology of the Egyptians of 4,000 years ago. Your taxi deposits you before a great expanse of sand intersected with mountainous pieces of glittering rock. Hieroglyphics on stones tell where the various sarcophagi and obelisks were cut for the different pharaohs. Others show where steles and statues have been cut. Most interesting is the 'unfinished obelisk', an enormous piece of work over 134 feet (41m) long, which lies still attached to a great mass of granite. You can walk along its length. No obelisk standing today is as long as this one. During the XVIIIth Dynasty, while it was being wrought, it developed a large crack on one side. Efforts to reduce its size revealed further flaws and it was abandoned.

High Dam

The dam and its dome-shaped exhibition building are well worth a visit if you are impressed by huge man-made structures. The hydroelectric generators within the dam provide most of Egypt's electricity. Its full generating capacity has not yet been reached. Indeed, the low level of the Nile has recently been a great source of worry to Egypt, causing shortage of generating capacity, insufficient irrigation water and levels too low in some locks to handle the larger Nile cruisers. Egypt is now even more dependent on the Nile than it was before.

Philae Temples ✓

As the temples on the island of Philae were already partly submerged by the waters behind the old dam, the Egyptian government decided they had to be moved when the High Dam was built, and, with the assistance of UNESCO, they were resited. A coffer dam was placed round the island and water pumped out. The temples were then painstakingly dismantled and removed to another island where they would be above the water line, so you now see them on Agilkia Island exactly as they were. The larger one, flanked by colonnades, is dedicated to Isis and her son Horus. The smaller one, dedicated to Hathor, has musical scenes with the cheerful little god Bes playing musical instruments. In one he plays a lute, and in another he is dancing with a tambourine. There is a nightly *son et lumière* show.

◆◆◆
ABU SIMBEL ✓

A visit to the rock-cut temples at Abu Simbel is often included in package tour cruises as an optional extra. The quickest way to travel the 174 miles (280km) from Aswân is by an EgyptAir flight, of which there are several each day. It is quite feasible to do the round trip in a day. There is also a daily bus which leaves from the town centre each morning, returning in the late afternoon.

The Abu Simbel temples were moved by a consortium of world powers to a new site, to avoid inundation beneath Lake Nasser when the High Dam was built, at a cost of 15 million pounds – and they are fantastic. So much has been written about them that, whether travellers are interested in temples or not, as one tourist poetically remarked:
'It is a status symbol
To visit Abu Simbel.'

The mighty resited temple of Ramses II at Abu Simbel

NILE CRUISING

The façade of the **Temple of Ramses II** is 108 feet (33m) high and 125 feet (38m) wide and is guarded by four seated figures of Ramses, each 65 feet (20m) high. There is a large door in the centre opened by a key of truly heroic proportions fashioned like the pharaonic *ankh* or Key of Life. This gives access to a great hall where eight more statues of Ramses, dressed as Osiris, soar into the vaulting. The ceiling is marvellously decorated and one wall depicts in panorama the pharaoh's battle with the Hittites at Qadesh. The most charming relief is of Ramses in his war chariot with his pet lion trotting by his side. A second hall has elaborately carved pillars and leads off into chambers and the inner sanctuary.

After visiting this temple and before going on to see the smaller one of Nefertari which Ramses built near by for his queen, there is another stop you must make. To the right of the main entrance there is a door which appears to go into the hillside. When you enter this you realise that the whole mountain into which the temple is set is false. In reality it is an enormous reinforced concrete dome, probably the largest in existence, which enfolds the temple. It is 400 feet (125m) high and 200 feet (60m) across at its base. Over it, sand and gravel has been spread to a depth of 6 feet (2m) so that, when viewed from outside, it looks like a natural mountain. It is a wonderful feat of engineering, fitted internally with pendula and strain gauges to indicate any movement or subsidence. The contrast between the exterior,

thousands of years old, and the stark modern interior, both in the middle of the desert, is astonishing.

After this you must see the second, smaller **Nefertari temple** with its lovely statues, pastel tinted walls and the Hathor figures with their strangely modern hairstyles. By now you may not be prepared to believe that these vast works could ever have been moved and you will certainly have seen no signs of it except for the dome itself. To understand exactly how and why the move was made you should spend a few minutes at the exhibition in Abu Simbel village where models and diagrams make it all clear to you. Some people prefer to see this first. You can also buy clay models of some of the finds here very reasonably.

To return to the temples: there are no official guides or dragomen. The entrance fee is fixed and the ticket covers not only an evening visit when the temples are floodlit inside and out, but also a second visit next day which can be at dawn as the sun's rays first strike.

Accommodation

Although the cruise traveller will have bed and board on the ship, some visitors may wish to stay longer in the main resorts along the Nile. Some hotels are described below.

Luxor

ETAP Luxor, Corniche el Nil Street (tel: 095 580944). To the north of the Luxor temple with all rooms facing the Nile. There are several shops in the lobby and

air-conditioned bungalows in the garden. 4-star
Jolieville Mövenpick Luxor, Crocodile Island (tel: 095 384855). A single storey bungalow village hotel set amongst palm trees and luxurious vegetation. Facilities include tennis courts, swimming pool and a jogging track; sailing and fishing can be arranged using *feluccas* and small boats. 5-star
Luxor Hilton (tel: 095 374933). At Karnak, close to the temple and city centre; 261 rooms and suites. 5-star
Luxor Sheraton, (tel: 095 374013). Magnificent views over the Nile. All facilities, plus nightclub; 298 rooms. 5-star
Philippe, Shari Nefertiti (tel: 095 372284). A clean, well-run hotel with roof-garden, swimming pool and Nile views. Good value for money. 3-star

Pullman Winter Palace, Corniche el Nil Street (tel: 095 580422). One of the grand 19th-century hotels; there is a beautiful garden with a large swimming pool, and very good cuisine. 4-star

Aswân
Amun, Amun Island (tel: 097 322555). On a small island in the river with a delightful garden. Here you can get away from it all and yet sail back to reality in minutes. 3-star
Amun Tourist Village, Sahara City (tel: 097 480439). A cottage-style complex 2 miles (3km) from the airport and upstream of the High Dam on Lake Nasser. There is a pool and a range of activities for guests such as camel-riding, minigolf and safari trips. 5-star
Aswân Oberoi, Elephantine Island (tel: 097 323455). This is

The Old Cataract Hotel, Aswân, is one of the loveliest hotels in Egypt

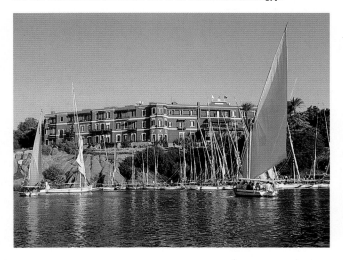

NILE CRUISING

Nile cruiser passing the Ptolemaic temple of Kom Ombo

the sort of place you dream about, quiet, restful and luxurious. You go over to the island on a ferry and the only noise is the singing of the birds for there are no cars. There is a small museum on the island. 5-star

Kalabsha, Abtal el Tahrir Street (tel: 097 322666). Situated behind the Cataract hotels, it has restaurant, bar and nightclub with folkloric entertainment and all the rooms are air-conditioned. 4-star

Old Cataract Pullman, Abtal el Tahrir Street (tel: 097 316002). Rich in beauty and atmosphere and served as a backdrop for the film *Death on the Nile*. A hotel beloved for nearly a century, on an ideal site above a curve in the Nile. 5-star

PLM Azur New Cataract, Abtal el Tahrir Street (tel: 097 323434). Shares the same 16-acre (6.5ha) garden, swimming pool and spectacular views as the 'old' Cataract but otherwise ultra modern. 5-star

Abu Simbel

There are two small 4-star hotels: the **Nefertari** (tel: 097 324836) is a comfortable hotel with modern conveniences and a swimming pool, set in the desert. It would be an oasis if one of the largest man-made lakes in the world, Lake Nasser, were not to hand. The bar at the Nefertari has a local Nubian atmosphere with native glass and basketwork décor. The **Nobaleh Ramses Hotel** (tel: 097 311660) also has a Ramses pub and a Nubian bazaar.

PEACE AND QUIET

Wildlife and Countryside
in Egypt
by Paul Sterry

Travel itineraries and destinations in Egypt are almost always centred on the Nile, since not only the capital, Cairo, but also most of the smaller cities lie close to the river's course. In a land which is largely desert, this influence is not surprising and, as a bonus to the visitor, the Nile is also the focal point for much of Egypt's wildlife. The river also had a profound effect upon the Egypt of the pharaohs, these past civilisations also relying on the bounty provided by the water. With a few notable exceptions, today's wildlife probably differs little from that depicted in the hieroglyphics: images of jackals, ibises, owls and bees are common and reflect the early significance of these creatures. Boat tours reveal fascinating and inspiring archaeological remains, and the stunning and evocative scenery along the banks of the Nile provides a wonderful setting for the river's wildlife. By way of contrast, a short trip into the desert reveals another side to Egyptian natural history: away from the influence of the Nile, water is at a premium and the animals survive some of the most arid conditions on earth.

In and Around Cairo
Despite the fact that nearly a quarter of Egypt's population lives in Cairo, making it one of the largest cities in the world, the wildlife of the urban areas and the surrounding land is still surprisingly varied. The Nile, which flows through the heart of the city, attracts waterbirds and migrants, and the proximity of ancient Egyptian relics on Cairo's desert fringes provides a unique blend of history and natural history. In spring and autumn, hundreds of thousands of birds which use the Nile as a route into and out of Africa, pass right over the centre of Cairo. Flocks of white pelicans wing their way overhead at dawn and dusk, sometimes in the company of white storks. Birds of prey, too, can be numerous and mixed groups of eagles and buzzards may be seen between March and May and again from August to October.

The shade and foliage provided by leafy gardens often attract migrant passerines to stop off and feed. Some, like the chiffchaff, may spend the winter here before returning to northern Europe. They join resident species like the charming and beautiful palm dove, also a frequent visitor to parks and gardens.

On both sides of the Nile, Cairo is bordered by desert and many routes radiate from the city into this inhospitable terrain. Driving along these will allow the visitor to see birds such as larks and wheatears and, after dark, there may even be a glimpse of a jackal. The Pyramids at Giza are on the itinerary of most visitors and the scrubby desert which surrounds these wonders is typical of much of Egypt. Because they are cold-blooded, reptiles benefit greatly from Egypt's almost guaranteed sunshine, and geckos and spiny-

PEACE AND QUIET

tailed lizards scurry among the rocks. The heat and lack of water can, however, prove a problem for birds and only the best-adapted species are found here. The Zoological Gardens and the nearby El-Urman Gardens are good spots to relax. They lie beside the Nile near the junction of Shari el Gîza and Shari Sarwat. Gîza and its surrounding desert is only 7½ miles (12km) from the centre of Cairo. It is best reached by taking a taxi from the city. All the roads that radiate from Cairo sooner or later pass through desert terrain.

The Nile
Running the entire length of Egypt, the Nile is Africa's longest river and, if its entire basin is taken into consideration, it is the longest river in the world. Although indisputably immense, its influence upon the lives of the inhabitants of Egypt past and present is out of all proportion to its size. Were it not for its presence in this most arid of countries, Egyptian civilisation probably would not have developed as it did.

> **Cattle Egret**
> Cattle egrets are a familiar sight along the banks, sometimes feeding in marshes and cultivated fields adjacent to the river. Flocks often gather at dusk to fly to roost and can even be seen winging their way over the centre of Cairo. As their name suggests, cattle egrets are often associated with grazing animals. They follow the hooves of cattle, snatching insects and reptiles disturbed by their passage.

The construction of the Aswân High Dam tamed the Nile and ended the seasonal flooding along its course, irrigation canals nowadays providing year-round supplies of water for agriculture. Gone too are the Nile crocodiles and Egyptian plovers which once haunted its banks, but it still hosts an amazing variety of wildlife. Pied kingfishers are numerous along the banks, sometimes hovering before plunge-diving

after fish into the waters below.
In undisturbed areas they nest
in holes in the river bank,
sharing this niche with little
green bee-eaters, which adorn
bushes and overhanging
branches.
Areas of exposed sand and
mud in the river offer feeding
grounds for migrant waders as
well as resident spur-winged
plovers, which are striking and
elegant birds. Do not expect to

*Spiny-tailed lizards haunt rocky
outcrops where they like to bask in
the sun*

be able to see the spurs on
their wings, however, since
these are only visible when the
bird is in flight, and then only at
close range, a combination of
circumstances which happens
rather infrequently! Egyptian
geese also haunt the quieter
shallows, especially where lush

PEACE AND QUIET

Egyptian geese are often seen in pairs, dabbling in shallow water

vegetation provides them with grazing, and small flocks are occasionally seen flying up and down the river in search of new feeding grounds.

Luxor
Built on the site of ancient Thebes, Luxor offers the visitor some of Egypt's finest antiquities and a wide variety of wildlife, all within a short distance of the town. Since it is situated on the Nile, water-loving birds are close to hand, but by way of contrast, the desert terrain surrounding many of the archaeological sites is bleak and arid. The landscape is often scarred, but far from diminishing the appeal of the desert creatures, this, together with the sense of history attached to the sites, only adds to the wildlife interest.
During migration time, parties of blue-cheeked bee-eaters, swallows and martins are frequently seen in the vicinity and sometimes stop to rest on convenient perches along the river banks.

The desert locust is migratory and sometimes found in Egypt's desert

Trumpeter Finch
One of the most characteristic species to be found around the Valley of the Kings is the trumpeter finch, a delightful little bird so-named because of its nasal call which sounds remarkably like a toy trumpet. When seen at close range they have subtle, pink plumage and a stubby red bill that looks as though it is made of plastic. The search for food is never-ending for birds who inhabit the desert and small parties of trumpeter finches are forever hopping among the stones and boulders and then suddenly flying off in search of a better feeding area.

Waders such as wood sandpipers and terns also pass through in some numbers and many stay for the winter.
On the west bank lies the Valley of the Kings, burial site for many of the great pharaohs, and near by is the Valley of the Nobles. The arid air which so suits the process of mummification renders the landscape bleak and barren and almost devoid of plant life. However, despite the harsh climate, a few plants and insects somehow manage to survive – food for a small but interesting variety of birds.

White-crowned black wheatears and a variety of larks favour this bleak terrain, often inconspicuous until they perch on a boulder or take to the wing. Overhead, resident Egyptian

vultures soar effortlessly on the
thermals, their numbers being
swollen in spring and autumn by
migrants. During the winter,
long-legged buzzards,
recognised by their unmarked,
rufous tails, become widespread
and are also seen around Luxor.

Aswân

Aswân is Egypt's southernmost
city, lying over 500 miles
(800km) south of Cairo. Like the
settlements further north it lies on
the banks of the Nile. Here, the
river is perhaps at its most
attractive: its wide course is
dotted with islands, some of
which can be visited, and the
elegant sailing barges known as
feluccas make good use of the
cooling breeze. The wildlife of
the river is also rich and varied,
while around the Aswân High
Dam, desert-loving species can
be seen.

Aswân's climate is at its most
equable from September to April
and a trip during this period
allows the visitor to see either
migrant birds in spring or

The Future of the High Dam
Although a remarkable testament
to man's determination and
ingenuity, the High Dam itself
and Lake Nasser beyond are
also a monument to his inability
to foresee the long-term
consequences of his actions.
The dam's prime importance as
a source of hydroelectric power
and irrigation is not in doubt,
but there are serious worries
that in many other ways it will
become an ecological disaster.
Sooner or later, it is feared, the
project will grind to a halt as the
waters of Lake Nasser rapidly fill
with the very silt which each
year used to travel north with
the flood waters to smother and
enrich the soils of the Nile Delta.
Because the waters are now
held back this no longer
happens, and as a consequence,
the level of soil in the Delta is
slowly but surely diminishing.
Not surprisingly, fertility of the
soil in the Delta has also been
reduced so that artificial
fertilisers now have to be used.

*Graceful feluccas line the banks of
the Nile at Aswân (above). Hooded
wheatears (right) can be found in the
surrounding desert*

autumn, or wintering species,
and sometimes even both. From
the banks of the Nile, gull-billed
terns can be seen, their elegant,
white plumage looking most
resplendent in the bright light.
White-winged black terns also
pass through Aswân in large
numbers, and flocks hawking
insects over the water with their
buoyant, graceful flight are a
memorable sight.

PEACE AND QUIET

The land surrounding the Aswân Dam is arid and desert-like but still supports a few interesting birds. Lanner falcons are occasionally seen patrolling the blue skies, while among the boulders and rocks, white-crowned black wheatears and hooded wheatears are always in residence. The latter species, with its black plumage with contrasting white crown, belly and chest must surely be one of Egypt's smartest birds.

The Nile at Aswân

Aswân is an ideal spot for those wanting a longer, relaxing break while travelling in Egypt. The drifting waters of the Nile are soothing to look at and also fascinating for the birdwatcher, and the many islands which lie in the river provide an interesting contrast to the city and the surrounding desert.

On the river, exposed sandbanks serve as roosts for terns and as feeding grounds for waders.

Considering the size of the Nile, however, it is not surprising that many of the best areas are distant, and for those without a telescope, what better way to get a good view than to hire a *felucca*? Wood, green and common sandpipers and greenshank can be numerous depending upon the time of year and there is always a chance of seeing a Senegal thick-knee. These curious birds, with large, yellow eyes and yellow legs are relatives of the stone-curlew, a bird of arid regions which is widespread in Egypt.

Islands in the Nile

If you hire a *felucca* for a whole day, it can be fascinating to visit two of the Nile's islands at Aswân. Elephantine Island, one of the largest accessible islands, is favoured by both wintering and migrant wheatears, larks and other passerines. By contrast, the smaller Botanic Island, which has lush vegetation, not only provides the visitor with welcome shade but also with the chance of seeing a different range of birds. Presented to Lord Kitchener as a gift when he was Consul-General of Egypt, the island is a haven of native and exotic plants from around the world, plants which its owner introduced to further his interest in botany.

Around the shore of the island, cattle egrets nest in the trees, flying off to feed in the shallows of the river and on cultivated land. Among the trees and shrubs, over-wintering chiffchaffs search for insects, often in the company of spectacled warblers

Elephantine Island (left) and nearby Botanic Island are good spots for migrant birds such as this chiffchaff (below)

and elegant Nile valley sunbirds. Bluethroats forage on the ground for insects and during migration time the bushes harbour a wide variety of warblers, wheatears and shrikes.

El Faiyûm

Just under 60 miles (100km) to the southwest of Cairo lies the settlement of El Faiyûm, home to over a million people. As Egypt's largest oasis, it is a region of cultivated land with lush irrigation canals, dominated by Birket Qârûn, a large lake formerly fed directly by the waters of the Nile. Both the margins of the lake and the fields and ditches surrounding it support a wealth of birdlife, although, sadly, the waters of Birket Qârûn are drying and becoming less attractive as the years go by.

The Changing Face of El Faiyûm
Man's influence on El Faiyûm dates back to the days of the pharaohs. The level of the lake, which once occupied a far greater area including most of the land today under cultivation, was gradually lowered by reducing the inflow from the Nile. The reclaimed land was soon cultivated and is now irrigated by a complex series of canals and ditches. The result is a region where a range of crops can be harvested throughout the year and sugar cane, figs, citrus fruits, olives, peppers and other vegetables are commonly grown and frequently seen on street stalls.

The dwindling margins of Birket Qârûn do not hold out much hope for its future importance to wildlife, but for the present its shores, and in particular those around the southeastern edge, are a wonderful haunt for waders. Passage birds such as sandpipers and ruffs mingle with avocets, black-winged stilts and spur-winged plovers and one of Egypt's most endearing birds, Kittlitz's plover, can also be seen around the shores of the lake. This dainty little wader, with a disproportionately large head and long legs, runs frantically over the mud pausing occasionally to snatch an item of food. Overhead, collared pratincoles and marsh terns hawk for the abundant insect life that the lake supports. Overgrown canals and ditches are a haven for frogs and also for secretive birds like little bitterns and purple gallinules, which are best seen either by patient watching or when they are suddenly disturbed. Nile valley sunbirds forage for insects among the foliage and fan-tailed warblers announce their presence with their 'zit-zit-zit' calls delivered in a bouncing song flight. Birket Qârûn is 10 miles (16km) north of El Fayûm. Leave Cairo on the Pyramids road and turn right at Mena House Oberoi.

Wadi Natrûn

A little over 60 miles (100km) to the northwest of Cairo, Wadi Natrûn has long been known for its monasteries and is a popular destination for tourists. It lies within a day's journey from the capital and the fields, scrub and lakes of the area harbour a wide variety of birds which provide a pleasant diversion from the

PEACE AND QUIET

Kittlitz's plover is a speciality of Birket Qârûn and Wadi Natrûn

historical interest of the buildings. Wadi Natrûn lies in a valley much of which is actually at or below sea level, and the series of seasonally fluctuating lakes were at one time a source of natron (sodium sesquicarbonate) during the summer months, from which the area got its name. Natron was vital in the mummifying process. Since they are situated in the middle of the desert, it is not surprising that the lakes attract a variety of migrant birds which pause here from their travels across the Sahara. Most noticeable are the waders and terns that stop off on passage in spring and autumn. With Birket Qârûn, this is one of the few areas in Egypt where there is a chance of seeing the delightful and diminutive Kittlitz's plover.

The drying margins of the lakes and the scraps of vegetation that surround them are also attractive to resident desert birds. Trumpeter finches, desert larks, short-toed larks and possibly even lesser short-toed larks are sometimes observed, while spotted sandgrouse on the other hand, are more often heard than seen. Despite their comparatively large size, they are difficult to spot and the musical calls of flocks in flight are often the only clue as to their whereabouts. Brown-necked ravens can also be located by their loud cawing calls. Do not

PEACE AND QUIET

Migrant painted lady butterflies are great travellers, and sometimes visit garden plants

expect to be able to see their brown necks, however, since they are only visible at close range.

Shrubs and bushes here and elsewhere in the cultivated Nile Delta are home to one of north Africa's most interesting and distinctive birds, the Senegal coucal. It prefers to live in the vicinity of water and, although generally shy, is often disturbed from cover or seen flying across the road, its rufous wings and long tail catching the eye. Wadi Natrûn can be reached by driving northwest from Cairo for 60 miles (100km) on the road to Alexandria.

Desert Life

For most of the year it seldom rains in Egypt. What little rain there is, is soon soaked up by the parched soil and so, away from the influence of the Nile, the land

Sandy deserts are a hostile environment to most animals

is barren and almost featureless desert. By comparison with the lush landscape beside the Nile and the richness of Egypt's antiquities, this environment may sound rather uninspiring. However, for many people, the desert exercises a unique kind of magic if only in arousing wonder at how its birds and mammals ever survive.

For the most part, Egypt's deserts are not the rolling sand

dunes which mention of the Sahara so vividly conjures up. Rather, they are stony and dusty with jagged outcrops of rock. From the point of view of the naturalist this is the more rewarding type of desert, since this habitat offers far more opportunities for life to survive. Here and there throughout the desert, there are a few oases with permanent water, but although these act like a magnet for some species, most true desert animals are so well adapted to life with little water that they have no need to visit waterholes. In places, seasonal streams, which for most of the year run dry, periodically flow down from the hills. Where a valley bottom contains scraps of shrubby vegetation, this may indicate that the stream flows underground and, although no water may be visible, the seeds from the plants and the insects they support attract a variety of birds.

Hoopoe larks are characteristic of this region, being easily recognised by their fluting song, long, down-curved bills and striking black and white wing bars.

Beautifully marked sand partridges call from low, rocky outcrops, the song sounding like stones being knocked together, and they too feed on the few seeds and insects that the desert provides.

Many of the desert's animals are largely nocturnal, thus avoiding the heat of the day, and towards dusk, cream-coloured coursers and stone curlews are sometimes disturbed close to roads. Scorpions and snakes which during the day seek refuge under boulders and in rock crevices, venture out in search of food. Drive from Cairo in almost any direction and you will encounter desert terrain eventually. For example, drive on the Pyramids Road and continue towards Bawati or turn south towards El Faiyûm.

Migration

Many of the birds which breed in Europe and Asia are only resident during the summer months, retreating south before the onset of winter to escape the cold and to find better feeding grounds. For some species this means flying south of the equator into southern Africa and for almost all it necessitates crossing the Sahara. Some fly directly over this inhospitable region, but many, and in particular water-loving birds like pelicans, ducks and waders, choose to follow the course of the Nile down through East Africa to their wintering grounds. This option not only offers a ready-made navigational aid but also provides an opportunity for feeding and

Male sand partridges sometimes call from exposed perches

Egyptian vultures are common on spring and autumn migration

watering stops *en route*.
Both spring and autumn
migration are good in Egypt,
with the months of March to May
and August to October being
especially varied. Flocks of sand-
martins and swallows are often
the first to appear in spring, the
numbers swelling those of the
year-round residents. House-
martins too are common on
migration, flocks of several
hundred sometimes gathering
over the water to catch insects.
Many species of waders pass
through the Nile region and,
since they tend to migrate at
night, small parties of spotted
redshanks and wood and marsh
sandpipers are sometimes seen
feeding during the daytime. By
contrast, bee-eaters, which pass
through Egypt in considerable
numbers, migrate during the day
and roost at night. These
incredibly colourful birds often
stop to perch on overhead wires
and branches and their

attractive, bubbling call quickly
draws attention to them. Because
they rely to a large extent on
thermals rising off the hot ground
to assist them in flight, birds of
prey also migrate by day. One of
the most striking of these to pass
along the course of the Nile is the
Egyptian vulture which, although
resident in its namesake country
in small numbers, is much more
common on passage. Its striking
black and white wings are easily
recognised and at close range its
wedge-shaped tail and almost
bare head are characteristic
features. Other migratory raptors
include Montagu's harrier, lesser
spotted eagle and steppe eagle,
the latter an elegant, uniformly
brown eagle which is sometimes
seen perched in low bushes or
even on the ground.

Ras Muhammad and the Red Sea
Sandwiched between the Gulf of
Suez and the Gulf of Aqaba, the

PEACE AND QUIET

Bee-keeping in Egypt

The earliest known records of bee-keeping are provided by Egyptian hieroglyphics dating back 3,500 years. These depict not only individual bees (the bee was often associated with royalty), but also the cylindrical clay hives in which traditional bee-keepers still keep their colonies today.

As pollinating insects, bees are vital for the success of many of Egypt's crops and today's agriculture requires modern bee-keeping practices with the bees' role as pollinators taking precedence over their honey-producing capacity. For smaller, more traditional farmers, however, the stacks of hives still provide a rich source of food and a valuable financial asset.

It was while managing their beehives that the ancient Egyptians first made use of the 'Plimsoll line' notion. Barges full of hives were set to drift northwards on the swelling Nile, as its seasonal floodwaters pushed towards the Mediterranean. With their progress, the surge in water level induced flowering along the Nile's banks, the hives gradually being filled with honey. When reached, the 'Plimsoll line', marked on the side of the barge, indicated that the hives were full and the honey ready for harvesting.

The seas and coral reefs around Ras Muhammad are a paradise for underwater exploration

Sinai peninsula is a land of contrast and beauty. Inland, there are baking deserts and freezing mountains, while the warm waters of the coast are a holiday-maker's dream. At the southernmost tip of the peninsula, where the two gulfs meet at the mouth of the Red Sea, lies Ras Muhammad with excellent views of the Red Sea mountains. Although only recently accessible to tourists, the seas off the coast have long been known in diving circles to harbour some of the finest coral reefs in the world.

Ironically, the increased interest in the natural wonders of the seas around Ras Muhammad is also contributing to its decline, as pollution and disturbance of the coral take their toll. However, with care and consideration there is still plenty that can be seen without causing undue harm to the environment.

Experienced divers can explore the edge of the reef where the abundance, variety and colour of the fish is absolutely staggering. Sabre squirrel fish, puffer fish, and shoals of black-spotted grunts and hatchet fish all patrol the open water around the coral, and moray eels, with their extraordinary heads, lurk in crevices and caves.

Training and equipment is available for novices and even inexperienced divers with snorkels can see a fascinating variety of fish, anemones and crabs close to the shore. Jutting out into the Red Sea, Ras Muhammad also provides an excellent spot for the birdwatcher. Particularly during periods of onshore winds, Cory's shearwaters can be seen offshore, flying on stiffly held wings in long lines known as rafts. Brown boobies nest further down the coast of the Red Sea. They resemble gannets, and have plumage that is principally brown, with white underparts. The rarer red-billed tropicbirds quickly attract attention.

In deeper water, Caspian terns plunge-dive in search of fish; closer to the shore sooty and white-eyed gulls catch fish and invertebrates and scavenge meals. Both species often associate with each other and nest on offshore islands. Although superficially similar in appearance to and outnumbered by sooty gulls, white-eyed gulls are distinctive and easy to recognise with their neatly defined white eyelids, black hood and deep red bill. In breeding plumage, they must surely be one of the world's most elegant gulls.

FOOD AND DRINK

The Egyptians love good food and have many special dishes. An Arabic proverb says: 'The amount of food eaten shows the regard in which the guest holds the host'; you are invariably pressed to eat more food than you can – but it is quite polite to refuse. Be assured it will not be wasted. Hospitality is traditional even in the desert, where the stranger is 'the guest of Allah'. For those who prefer to eat the food they are used to at home, hotels and restaurants are the answer. If you wish to sample the local dishes, their Arabic names are often spelt phonetically for tourists. Here are a few:

Kebab: lamb cut into cubes, rubbed with lemon juice and olive oil, threaded on skewers and grilled over charcoal.

Shwarma: lamb grilled on a vertical spit, sliced and eaten between two flat unleavened loaves.

Mezza: Middle East *hors d'oeuvres*, which includes stuffed vine leaves, olives, small onions, etc.

Kofta: spicy ground lamb rolled into sausage shape and threaded on skewers, often interspersed with kebab.

Ta'maia: bean cakes deep fried in boiling oil. Can be bought on street corner stalls.

Fool: a concoction of simmered beans served with Arabic bread, often for breakfast.

Samak: fish and shellfish. Plentiful and delicious; both from the Nile and Mediterranean.

Baclava: many layers of thin dough interleaved with crushed nuts and sugar. Honey is poured over the pastry when it comes from the oven.

Shai: tea, usually served in a glass.

Karkaday: a Nubian speciality,

A tempting display of Egyptian pastries

FOOD AND DRINK

brewed from hibiscus blossoms
and served hot or cold.
Assir: fresh fruit juice: lemon,
mango, guava or orange.
Doum: an Aswân drink like fruit
juice, made from the heart of the
palm tree.
Stella beer: enjoyed by tourists
and rather similar to Belgian
Stella Artois. Usually in large
bottles, sufficient for one large or
two lesser thirsts.

Eating Out

Most restaurants and cafés can
produce European food but, if
you order familiar things, it is as
well to remember that beef can
be tough, veal is scarce and pork
is not popular in a Muslim
country. However, in the luxury
and first class hotels frozen
meats are imported. The best
local meat by far is lamb.
Chicken and fish are also a good
choice. Vegetables and fruit are
usually fresh and of good quality.
If you wish to be adventurous
and do not speak Arabic it is
easy to point to things in open-

*At Groppi's: this old Cairo café is
famous for its ice cream*

fronted cafés, many of which
have legs of lamb on a spit
constantly turning.
Egyptian bread is unleavened
and therefore does not rise. It is
shaped in flat thin rounds and,
torn in two, makes a delicious
sandwich especially with a slice
of lamb from the spit. Don't
worry about taking a whole loaf;
it is hollow and not as filling as it
looks.
If you want a picnic or a quick
snack you can go into a café and
order meat or cheese in Arabic
bread and there is no need for
knives or forks or plates. In
hotels it is often torn in two and
crisped in the oven to make
Melba toast.
For Egyptians, the main meal is
lunch, which is taken between
13.00 and 16.00hrs. However,
the more tourist-conscious
establishments serve substantial
evening meals.

FOOD AND DRINK

Egyptians are very fond of fish. In pharaonic times they enjoyed mullet, carp, perch, tigerfish and eel. They knew how to dry and salt fish and even had an early version of tartar sauce, made from the juice of sour grapes. Many people claim the Mediterranean fish is not as tasty as that from colder waters, but it depends how quickly it is cooked. Nothing can be nicer than trout caught and grilled immediately with a little butter. It tastes even better if you have just caught it yourself! There are a number of fish restaurants and it is difficult to say where giant prawns *en broche* taste the best. Two places in Cairo which are particularly worth a try are the Sea Horse and Good Shot on the outskirts of Maadi, overlooking the Nile.

Desert Feasts

To be a guest at a desert feast is an unusual experience which can sometimes be included in a tour or arranged independently. The *pièce de résistance* is invariably a whole sheep roasted over a barbecue pit until the meat is thoroughly cooked and crispy outside. There are often many guests, and they sit cross-legged on thick, hand-woven carpets or cushions at low tables. Whether the feast is in a tent or under palm trees, it is customary to remove your shoes. First the roast mutton is displayed on a great platter for all to see and admire, and other large dishes are produced, some with mounds of saffron-coloured rice covered with pine kernels. Sometimes forks and knives are used, sometimes not. If not, it is quite easy to eat with your fingers, dipping pieces of bread into the various dishes, putting pieces of meat in your mouth and then making small balls of rice and doing likewise. Only the right hand should be used; it is regarded as unclean to use the left hand, which attends to personal hygiene! Finger bowls will be produced to wash your fingers later. The meat course will be followed by sweet dishes and fruit.

The coffee or tea which finishes the feast is poured with much ceremony. Sometimes the coffee pot may be two or three feet (up to a metre) tall, yet the coffee pourer (who is not chosen, but offers his services as he has mastered the art and enjoys it) has to hold the pot high in the air above the tiny cup or glass and pour it without spilling a drop. After you drink the first cup it is filled again with the same *élan*. You may refuse the third cup. Should the beverage be tea, the first cup will be sweet, the second sweeter and the third sweetest of all. Coffee is often served with cardamom seeds, which give it a spicy flavour.

Wine

Winemaking in Egypt dates back as far as records exist. The vine was imported from Asia and wine was ascribed to the gods – in Egypt to Osiris; there were also special funerary wines. In the 7th century, the Arabs swept through Egypt and, as their religion forbade wine, viticulture declined. More recently, the demand for wine, especially by visitors, has caused it to be reintroduced on a commercial scale. The venture was begun at the end of the last century by a Greek named Gianaclis and the huge vineyards of today outside Alexandria still bear his name. They extend over 20,000 acres (8,094ha), including five villages for the workers. The vines are on flat, sandy soil, instead of the more usual terraces of Europe. They are watered about five times a year during the growing season by the simple process of flooding. The sun does the rest. Each section is protected from the desert winds by windbreaks of pine trees.

The range, from the driest to the sweetest white, is Clos Matamir, Gianaclis Villages, Crus des Ptolemées, Nefertiti and Reine Cleopatra. The most popular red is Omar Khayyam, rather like a Chianti. Local wines are readily available in most hotels, and are reasonably priced. French and Italian wines are much more expensive.

SHOPPING

Shops throughout Egypt sell international goods as well as Egyptian ones. Most of the department stores are in Cairo, and situated in the city centre. Nearly all display price tags, and prices are not subject to bargaining. But few visitors can resist the bazaars, where bargaining takes place with good humour. You can buy the famous *mushrabia*, plain or inlaid with

The bazaar in Luxor. Haggling is part of the shopping experience

SHOPPING

mother of pearl and ivory. There is copper and brass ware, and gold and silver jewellery – the latter often sold by weight rather than design, so that prices are reasonable.

The jewellery includes lustrous strings of freshwater pearls, sometimes entwined with onyx or coral. Wallets of real leather and handbags, including snake skin, are of individual design, and very reasonably priced. Museum reproductions include statues of the gods, such as the cat goddess Bast.

Bedouin rugs woven of camel or goat hair, plain or patterned, are difficult to resist and can be rolled up and tied to bring home although, unfortunately, when undone, they won't disgorge a beautiful Cleopatra, as happened in Caesar's case! Hand-loomed cotton rugs for hallways are lighter and cheaper. Hand-carved walking sticks are unusual and easy to carry, as is basketwork. Antique wine tables and other small pieces of furniture are beautifully inlaid with mother of pearl, ivory and different woods set in lead. Due to the danger of lead poisoning, this craft is now forbidden.

It is still possible to find hand-crafted goods in street markets

Beware of fake antiques, especially amulets said to have been taken from ancient tombs. It is sometimes difficult to distinguish the fake from the genuine, as many are made with the same artistry as in pharaonic times. But then you might argue that, if they are beautifully crafted and give you pleasure, it doesn't matter whether they were made yesterday or centuries ago. Beware of street traders offering obvious trash.

ACCOMMODATION

Egypt has been known for its luxurious hotels since tourism became popular in the 1880s. A few of these splendid edifices remain, such as the **Cataract** in Aswân and the **Winter Palace** in Luxor, both of which have added modern annexes. In recent years a number of the international chains have built hotels, among them Sheraton, Hilton, Marriott, Pullman and Ramada, with pools,

entertainment, shops and international menus. Classifications range from 5-star down to 1-star, and in the former guests can expect to pay well over $100 a night in Cairo for a double room (less in Upper Egypt). Higher rates apply to rooms facing the Nile. Last minute bookings of rooms is not unusual, though getting a room facing the Nile may be difficult.

CULTURE, ENTERTAINMENT AND NIGHTLIFE

Of the night entertainments the most fascinating are the *son et lumière* performances at the Gîza Pyramids, Karnak temple in Luxor and Philae temple in Aswân. Daily English-language newspapers and monthly magazines give details of the performances given in different

Horse-drawn carriage (garry) at the Pullman Winter Palace, Luxor

ENTERTAINMENT

languages. They also carry the addresses of fashionable nightclubs and houseboats moored along the Nile banks where you can dine quietly and well and see a cabaret.

Two well-known companies to look out for are the National Ballet and the Reda Group, who do folkloric dancing and are often on television.

Nightclubs and discothèques are reasonably priced; it depends on what and how much you drink. Most hotels have cabarets with oriental orchestras and belly dancers. If you wish to have an unusual night out, some travel agencies can arrange a tent party with cabaret and dinner and sometimes horse dancing displays; and Dervish

A belly dancer is obligatory in an Egyptian cabaret show

dancers, who are hypnotic to watch, often perform. They skilfully manipulate tambourines and castanets, make swooping movements and whirl or spin continuously, so that their embroidered robes float out horizontally as if fixed in space. The Enlgish language daily paper *The Egyptian Gazette* and the monthly magazine *Egypt Today* will have details on these and other entertainments. Your hotel hall porter will also advise you.

WEATHER AND WHEN TO GO

It seldom rains in Egypt, but you may experience a *khamseen*, when hot winds pick up sand in the desert and distribute it everywhere, and the sky clouds over. The *khamseen* does not generally last long and there are rarely more than half-a-dozen a year; but it is best to stay indoors until it passes.

Nothing can enhance a holiday more than good weather and in Egypt it is almost predictable. Most days are warm and sunny, with the added attraction that the temperature drops considerably at night, even during the summer.

Autumn and winter have in the past been the preferred times for Europeans and Americans to visit, when the days are crisp and sunny and the nights cool; but today, with air-conditioning everywhere, tourism flourishes all year round.

What to Pack

Obiviously take into account the time of year you will travel; but a few personal tips here can

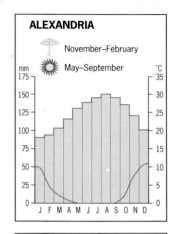

ALEXANDRIA
November–February
May–September

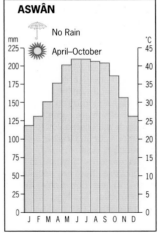

ASWÂN
No Rain
April–October

make all the difference to your visit. A cardigan, wool sweater or light waterproof will be useful at night. Low walking shoes are a must, but not sandals, as they let in the sand. Sunglasses are helpful at any time of year and, although some tourists prefer to go bare-headed,

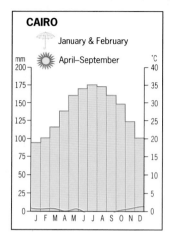

CAIRO

January & February

April–September

it is strongly recommended that you wear a sun-hat. If you have no room to pack one they can be bought anywhere. Binoculars – even small ones – are invaluable, especially whilst on the Nile. When visiting tombs and temples, which are sometimes ill lit, a torch will enable you to return for a second look at something special.

Should you forget anything in the way of dress, there are excellent shops and most hotels have their own boutiques. Clothing and shoes are very reasonable in price. When dining in the evening ladies usually wear cocktail dresses and men ties, but this very much depends on where you are.

Women tourists should never enter mosques wearing sleeveless low-necked dresses, mini skirts or shorts. If you are carrying a head scarf, it shows respect to wear it when you are in the mosque.

HOW TO BE A LOCAL

● The majority of Egyptians are followers of Islam, but there is a Coptic Christian minority. One way to recognise the latter is by their names, which will be more familiar to the ear than Arabic ones.

● The locals are cheerful, hospitable and will wish to please you. Show respect for their customs. Do not kiss or show affection in public. Never forget to remove your shoes when entering mosques. Women should cover their heads and not wear scanty clothing.

● Time means little to locals, which can be annoying but must be tolerated. A Spaniard enquiring if there was an Arabic equivalent of *mañana* was given the reply, 'we have no word which conveys quite that sense of urgency'!

● A great many Egyptians speak English. They love the telephone and hate to write letters. They spend hours on the telephone (local calls cost nothing), and are becoming keen on fax machines.

● The *galabieh* is still very much in evidence. It is a practical dress for a hot climate, but you will also see denims and jackets in the streets these days.

● Bargaining is a way of life, and you will earn only contempt if you pay the asking price for most things in bazaars and small shops. It is considered a game and is conducted quite light-heartedly. Start with less than half the asking price and be prepared to walk away. Generally give the impression that you do not care.

The local scene in a busy street in Aswân

- If you are a guest and like something you see, think twice before saying so. Your host may feel bound by convention to ask you to take it. Do not be surprised by the amount of food that is produced. You will be pressed to eat, but it is quite polite to refuse. Rest assured that nothing will be wasted when the remains disappear from the table.

SPECIAL EVENTS

Horse and camel racing are popular throughout the year, and are sometimes held on the golf course at Gîza. Duck shooting in the Faiyûm Oasis takes place during the migration season. Sporting clubs offer temporary membership to visitors.
The following list gives an idea of the range of events taking place.

February
Hurghada, Red Sea: International Fishing Festival

Cairo: Arab Horse festival
March
Nasr City, Cairo: Cairo International Fair
April
South Sinai: Sinai Festival
May
Cairo: Nile Swimming Race
Alexandria: Weight-lifting Festival
July
Hurghada, Red Sea: Local Fishing Festival
August
Cairo: International Judo Festival
September
Ismailia: International Folklore Festival
Canal Long Distance Swimming Race
December
Cairo: International Cinema Festival
Cairo/Luxor/Aswân: International Rowing Race

CHILDREN

The **Cairo Zoo** is an endless joy.
There are marine aquaria with
amazing and exotic fish, and
camel rides are particularly
popular. In Cairo the **Heliopolis
Kids Club** meets monthly at the
Baron Heliopolis Hotel, usually on
the last Friday of each month.
Children aged from 4 to 14 of
different nationalities share in
games, programmes, lunch and
entertainments (tel: 02 2912468).
Children can also enjoy
museums such as the **Railway
Museum** adjoining Cairo Railway
Station and **Dr Ragab's
Pharaonic Village** on Jacob
Island.

TIGHT BUDGET

Travel Travelling independently
in Egypt can involve hassles, but
there are rewards for the
adventurous. To help keep costs
down, here are some tips:
Accommodation There are
some cheap 1- and 2- star hotels,
but standards of cleanliness are
dubious; check with a local
tourist office. Alternatively, try
the Cairo Youth Hostel at Abdul
Aziz al Saoud, Roda Island
(tel: 02 840729), or the
Association of Tourist Friends at
33 Qasr el Nil Street, Cairo (tel:
02 8922036). Camping in the
desert is not an option.
Food Eat cheaply in local
restaurants by choosing local
food and drinking coke or beer.
The round flat bread is
subsidised.
Entertainment Visit local street
markets, where the customer/
vendor haggling is fun to watch –
and can be instructive, too! Or
buy a balcony seat at the cinema
where western films are often
shown.
Shopping Buy cheap trinkets as
presents, but remember always
to bargain. Film can be bought
cheaply, but avoid hotel shops
where it is expensive. Clothing
and shoes are also cheap, and
can be made to measure.

A camel trek can be fun

DIRECTORY

Arriving

Cairo International Airport is
14 miles (23km) from the city
centre. If you are not met by a
tour operator or friends there are
plenty of taxis or coaches to take
you into town. Should you have
to wait there are restaurants and
cafeterias and, of course, banks if
you want to change money.
English is spoken by many
airport staff and there are Tourist
Police to help you. They wear
white uniforms in summer and
black in winter. Outbound or
return flights should be
confirmed through your hotel or
travel agent 72 hours before
departure.
All tourists need a passport valid
for six months beyond their visit,
and also a visa, available from
Egyptian consulates abroad or,
in emergencies, on arrival at
Cairo Airport.
You can take your car to Egypt
from Bari or Venice; contact
Adriatica Lines (in London tel:
0171 488 9821). A carnet and an
international driving permit are
needed to transport cars. Cars
with diesel-powered engines are
not allowed in.
You are required to register with
the police and have your
passport stamped within one
week of arrival. Hotels normally
do this for you but, if staying
privately, you must do this
yourself.

Camping

This is becoming increasingly
popular and there are a number
of sites especially along the sea
coasts. Most campsites are in the
Sinai on the north (Mediterranean)
and south (Red Sea) coasts.

You can obtain a detailed list
from tourist offices (for
addresses, see **Tourist Offices**,
below).

Crime

Crime is not a serious problem.
Walking at night is reasonably
safe in city centres. Pickpockets
are prevalent in crowds, so take
care when carrying money or
valuables. Keep car boots locked
– traffic lights are lucrative
places for thieves.

Customs Regulations

Personal effects, cameras,
radios, typewriters, tape or video
recorders and jewellery are
exempt from duty but may be
listed on a declaration form. The
original is retained by Customs
and you are given the duplicate
in case it is needed to facilitate
departure.
Duty free allowances are: 200
cigarettes or 25 cigars or 200g of
tobacco, 3 litres of spirits, 1 litre
of perfume and up to £E500
worth of gifts. Cash, travellers'
cheques and gold in excess of
£E500 must be declared. Only
£E1000 in local currency can be
taken into or out of Egypt. You
can have access to the duty free
shop on arrival, before going
through Customs.

Disabled Visitors

In Cairo, the Nile and Ramses
Hiltons and the Novotel have
facilities for disabled visitors, and
Oasis (Cairo) and Jolieville
(Luxor) are also recommended
by the Egyptian Tourist Office.
Etams Tours, at 13 Kasr el Nil
Street, 3rd Floor, Apartment 8,
Cairo (tel: 02 754721/752462)
specialises in tours and
sightseeing plus accessible

DIRECTORY

accommodation for disabled
people (for example, it offers
'Oases' and 'Valley of the Kings'
tours).

Driving
Driving is on the right and is
certainly not recommended for
the faint-hearted, especially in
Cairo! Petrol is cheap and
widely available in cities and
towns, but less so in the
countryside. Road signs are in
English in Cairo and the main
cities, but often only in Arabic
elsewhere. Several maps of
Egypt are available, but large
scale detailed ones and town
plans are hard to find. The
Automobile and Touring Club of
Egypt has a club premises for
purely social purposes in Cairo.
It does not offer recovery, legal
or insurance services, but will
assist with the temporary
importation of private cars. Its

At the Cairo bus station

address is 10 Qasr en Nil Street,
Cairo (tel: 02 743355).

Car Breakdown The telephone
number for an emergency is 142.
There is no motoring association
aid or private recovery system;
this is done by the Traffic Police.

Car Rental Self-drive and
chauffeur driven cars are
available for hire. In Cairo, Hertz,
Avis and Budget are represented
at the major hotels.
Arrangements may also be made
through airlines. To hire a car a
driver must be over 25 and have
an international driving permit. A
minimum deposit or credit card
is needed. Check that you are
adequately insured.

Desert Driving Even on main
roads this is hazardous; away
from them, it can be deadly. You
need special permission to make
detours, which should not be
attempted by most motorists.
Always carry as much spare
water (for car and passengers)
and fuel as possible, travel in
convoy, if lost do not leave your
vehicle. Anyone contemplating
desert driving should obtain
detailed information and contact
their motoring organisation first.

Electricity
Most of Egypt has 220 volt 50
cycle AC. Sockets are of the two
pin type, sometimes with an
earth connection. Power failures
are not unknown.

Embassies
Australia: Cairo Plaza Building,
5th and 6th floors, Corniche el
Nil, Cairo (tel: 02 777900).
Britain: Ahmed Raghab Street,
Garden City, Cairo (tel: 02
3540850).

Canada: 6 Mohammed Fahmy el Said, Garden City, Cairo (tel: 02 3543110).
USA: 5 Latin America Street, Garden City, Cairo (tel: 02 3557371).

Emergency Telephone Numbers
Police: 122
Fire/Ambulance: 125
The number for the Anglo-American Hospital, next to Cairo Tower, is 02 3406162. It is advisable to double-check all telephone numbers, as they are being changed.

Entertainment Information
Perhaps the most important of Cairo's night entertainments is the *son et lumière* spectacle at the Pyramids. Be sure to check on the language of the commentary before you go. There are also cinemas, several theatres and a brand new opera house, as well as several casinos

Travel first class on the Cairo-Aswân Express

and numerous nightclubs, several on the road to the Pyramids. Many hotels and restaurants offer Western-style shows, folk dancing and a belly dancer. These vary from the rustic to the artistic and you may well be roped in to take part! *Places* magazine is published every two months and distributed free through hotels, airlines and tourist offices (see also **Media**, below).

Health
Visitors arriving from a cholera or yellow fever infected area must have a certificate of inoculation. Check with your doctor on the current health situation; you may need protection against hepatitis A, polio, typhoid and possibly malaria.

DIRECTORY

It is most important to be careful what you eat and drink to avoid intestinal disorder. In a hot climate food deteriorates quickly. It is best to eat only fruit which you can peel. Cooked hot food is normally safer than cold; try to avoid salads. In case of illness there are very good hospitals in most towns and many hotels have a doctor on call. As Bilharzia is common it is safer to bathe only in swimming pools or the sea and not the Nile. Malaria is not very prevalent.

It is important to drink only bottled or mineral water, and not from the tap. It was not always so, but the great influx of people since the oil boom, Middle East conflicts and catastrophe in Lebanon has overloaded the system. Try not to take ice with your drinks unless you are certain it has been made with bottled or purified water. When out sightseeing many people carry a bottle of Baraka bottled water with them. Cola is often on sale at sites. Have it opened in front of you.

If you need to see a doctor, expect to pay on the spot for the consultation, plus the cost of any prescription.

Holidays

Exact dates for some of these holidays vary from year to year; latest details are available from tourist offices.

Union Day 22 February
Sinai Liberation Day 25 April
Sham al Naseem April/May
Labour Day 1 May
Bairam Feast Movable
Liberation Day 18 June
23 July Revolution 23 July
Nile Day August
Islamic New Year Movable
Prophet's Birthday Movable
Army Day 6 October
Victory Day 23 December
Bairam is the most important holiday of the year, lasting three days at the end of Ramadan (the Muslim month of fasting).

Lost Property

If you forget anything on a train, report the loss to the nearest stationmaster; if on an aircraft to the airline. If you lose anything in a hotel, staff are often willing to help look for it. Always ask. Airlines are good at tracing lost baggage and hotels will send on items left behind.

Media

Newspapers There are two English language newspapers, the *Egyptian Mail* and the *Egyptian Gazette*, the latter established in 1880. There is also the English-language monthly magazine *Egypt Today*, full of useful information on entertainments, restaurants, shopping and sightseeing.

Television and Radio As well as Arabic programmes, American and English shows are broadcast, so you can sometimes keep up to date with your favourite serials in your hotel room. There are several news bulletins in English on TV and radio. You can check the times in your newspaper, which is often delivered gratis with your hotel breakfast.

Money Matters

The Egyptian pound, represented by £E, is divided into 100 piastres. Although milliemes are no longer in circulation, price tags sometimes show three figures after the decimal point, eg 10.300, which is 10 pounds, 30 piastres. Bank note denominations are £E 1, 5, 10, 20 and 50. Piastres (Pt) are also in notes: 5, 10, 25 and 50. Coins are increasingly rare. Most hotels and restaurants take major credit cards. It is illegal to buy anything in any currency other than Egyptian pounds. There are bank offices in many of the bigger hotels.

Opening Times
Government and Public Sector Offices 08.30–14.30hrs (winter); 08.30–14.00hrs (summer); 10.00–14.00hrs, Sundays, Thursdays and Saturdays (Ramadan).
Public Sector Banks Monday to Thursday 08.30–13.00hrs; Sundays 10.00–12.30hrs; closed Fridays.
Private Sector Banks Mondays to Thursdays 09.00–13.00hrs; Sundays 10.00–14.00hrs; most banks closed Fridays and Saturdays.
Office Hours Mondays to Thursdays 09.00–16.00hrs; some offices close on Fridays, others on Sundays.
Shops Larger shops are open 08.30–12.30hrs and 16.00–19.00hrs. All are closed on Fridays, and many also on Sundays.

Personal Safety
It is essential to be careful crossing streets and *midans* (squares), especially in Cairo, as, although driving should be on the right, it is sometimes in the middle or on the left! Pedestrian crossings are usually observed but be careful not to trip on the uneven pavements.

When walking alone, keep to crowded and well-lit streets and dress inconspicuously.

Pharmacies
Pharmacies sell drugs, cosmetics and perfumes. Opening hours are about the same as other shops, except for night service stores which stay open all night. You will find them in most Egyptian towns. Here are some Cairo pharmacies:
Shubra Pharmacy, Massara Street (tel: 02 940782).
Bab el Sha'aria Pharmacy, Bab el Sha'aria Square (tel: 02 935151).
Ataba Pharmacy, Ataba Square (tel: 02 910831).
Isa'f Pharmacy, Ramses Street (tel: 02 743369).
Zamalek Pharmacy, 3 Shargaret el Dor Street (tel: 02 3402406).
Essam Pharmacy, 101 9th Street, Maadi (tel: 02 3504126).
Helwan Pharmacy, 17 Ahmed Anas Street (tel: 02 3508018).

Places of Worship
The majority of Egyptians are Muslims. Coptic Christians number about 8 million.
St Mark's Coptic Cathedral, 222 Ramses, Abbassiya (tel: 02 820681). This was rebuilt recently and a school of religious studies is attached to it.
All Saints Cathedral (Episcopal/ Anglican) is behind the Marriott Hotel in Zamalek (tel: 02 459391). Services in English.
St Joseph's Roman Catholic Cathedral is also in Zamalek (tel: 02 408902/3409348).
It is said that if a Muslim prayed in a different mosque in Cairo each day for a year he would not have entered all the mosques in the city.

DIRECTORY

Police

There are three main kinds of police: the Municipal Police, the Tourist Police and the Traffic Police.

The **Tourist Police** are on duty at Cairo Airport, the main railway station, Khan el Khalili and the Pyramids, and are ready to give assistance. They usually know two languages and are identified by an armband with 'Tourist Police' on it. Their head office is at 5 Adly Street (tel: 02 926028). Other offices: airport office, tel: 02 629584; Khan el Khalili office, tel: 02 904827; main railway station, Midan Ramses, tel: 02 764214; pyramids zone, Pyramids Road (opp Mena House Hotel), tel: 02 850259; Cairo Museum office, Midan Tahrir, tel: 02 754319.

The **Traffic Police** do their best to enforce speed limits throughout Egypt. Speeding outside cities is a serious offence which can attract heavy fines. The speed limits are 43mph (70kph) in towns and 56mph (90kph) elsewhere. Radar and motor cycle patrols are used, especially on the Desert and Delta roads to Alexandria.

Post Office

In Cairo the Central Post Office is open 24 hours a day. Other offices usually open 08.30–15.00hrs and are closed on Fridays. Letters up to 10g within Egypt cost Pt5. Airmail up to 10g to other Arab countries costs Pt15 and to Europe and the US £E1.

Public Transport

Air EgyptAir operates internal services to Alexandria, Luxor, Aswân, Abu Simbel, Al-Wadi al-Gadded, Hurghada, North and

Minarets and domes at sunset: modern Cairo seems a world away

South Sinai, the latter through an affiliate, Air Sinai (tel: EgyptAir 02 3902444; Air Sinai 02 760948).
Buses There is an extensive metropolitan network in Cairo comprising buses, metro, trains, river buses and taxis. A fairly comprehensive network of long-

distance buses, mostly air-conditioned and well organised, covers the rest of Egypt. Full particulars are available from tourist offices (see below).

Rail There is a frequent service between Cairo and Alexandria, and there are trains with sleeping cars to Upper Egypt. First class travel is recommended and a reservation should be made in advance. Classes below first are not recommended to anyone who would prefer a comfortable journey.

Taxis Taxis are reasonably priced and painted black and white in Cairo. The fare should be agreed in advance as meters are not to be relied upon. Do not be surprised if the driver gives a

DIRECTORY

Red post boxes for ordinary mail, green for express, blue for air mail

lift to a friend *en route*. It is an Egyptian custom and it would never occur to him to ask your permission!

Sea Many cruise ships call at Alexandria or traverse the Canal from Port Said to Suez. Nile cruises operate from Luxor and Cairo to Aswan.

You can cross the Red Sea from Hurghada to Sharm el Sheikh (Sinai) by regular services. For further information contact Sea Cruisers (tel: 065 446282) or ask your hotel.

Senior Citizens

Elderly tourists seem to thrive in Egypt, enjoying the dry sunny climate. It is advisable for them not to attempt too much in one day and, if possible, to take the early morning or afternoon tours, so avoiding the hottest part of the day. There are some special services for the elderly with tours including accommodation,

transportation and sightseeing by specially equipped buses, organised by **Etams Tours**, 13 Kasr El Nil, Cairo (tel: 02 745721).

Student and Youth Travel

More and more young people are coming to explore Egypt and see the sights by bus, train or on foot and do a Nile trip by *felucca*. The latter entails being prepared to 'rough it'. Meals are basic, the toilet is a bucket over the side and you spend the night on the bank in your sleeping bag. If you are prepared, it can be an unforgettable experience. There is camping at some places on the Mediterranean and Red Sea coasts (see **Camping** above) and a Youth Hostel organisation. (See also **Accommodation** page 109.) Leaflets from the tourist offices give details (see **Tourist Offices**, below).

Telephones

Long-distance and international calls are best made from public telephone offices, where you give a clerk the number you require and pay in advance for a specified time. For a surcharge, such calls can be made from up-market hotels but pay telephones with direct international dial capability are found in Cairo only. (Phone boxes are basically for local calls.)

Once connected to an international line, dial 00, then the country code, then the area code, then the number.

Time

Egypt is two hours ahead of Greenwich Mean Time and seven hours ahead of New York.

Tipping

Baksheesh (a tip) is almost universal in Egypt. Here is a rough guide to amounts. Porters: £E1; taxis: Pt50 for a short trip, more for a longer one. Many hotels and restaurants add a 12 per cent service charge, but an extra 5 per cent is usual for some special service.

A shopkeeper does not expect a tip but if, as often, you are offered tea, coffee or a soft drink, give a small tip to the person who serves it.

Baksheesh is a way of life in Egypt and is expected for any small service. Keep plenty of small notes readily to·hand.

Toilets

There is a dearth of public toilets and you will have to rely on hotels, restaurants and cafés.

Tourist Offices

London: 168 Piccadilly, London W1V 9DE (tel: 0171 493 5282).

Montreal: Place Bonaventure, 40 Frontenac, PO Box 304, Montreal, PQ H5A IB4 (tel: 014/861 4420).
New York: 630 Fifth Avenue, New York, NY 10111 (tel: 212/ 332 2570).

In Egypt there are offices in **Cairo** at 5 Adly Street (tel: 02 3913454); **Alexandria**, Said Zaghloul (tel: 03 4807611); **Luxor**, Nile Street (tel: 095 372215); **Aswân**, Tourist Bazaar (tel: 097 323297); **Port Said**, Palestine Street (tel: 066 223868).

A Nile cruise by felucca *is only for the hardiest tourists*

LANGUAGE

Arabic is Egypt's official
language, but many speak
English and French. At hotels,
airports and major shopping
areas, English is spoken as a
second language.
Useful words in Arabic, spelt
phonetically for pronunciation:
Yes aiwa
No la
How much becacm
Good day sa-eeda
Never mind maleesh
Please menfadlak
Thank you shookrun
Stop stanner shwyer
Little shwyer
Possible moomkin
Not possible moosh moomkin
That's all bus
Right yemeen
Left shemal
Money feloose
Give me edeenie
Bring me hatt
Here hinna
Listen isma
I do not have mafeesh
Taxi taxi
Bus autobus

Good kwice
Milk labban
Sugar sooker
Tea shy
Coffee ahwa
Water moya
Street sharia
Village ezba
If God is willing (often used for
yes) en sha allah

As there are only 10 numerical
signs to remember in Arabic, it is
worthwhile to learn them. This
will enable you to decipher bus
numbers and price tags in shops,
even if you only have them
written on a card.

1	WAHID	١
2	ETNEIN	٢
3	TALATA	٣
4	ARBAA	٤
5	KHAMSA	٥
6	SITTA	٦
7	SABBA	٧
8	TAMANYA	٨
9	TESSA	٩
10	ASHRA	١٠

*Temple relief at Karnak: Egypt's past
is still its greatest asset*

INDEX

128

ACKNOWLEDGEMENTS

Acknowledgements
The Automobile Association would like to thank the following
photographers and libraries for their assistance in the compilation of this
book:

AA PHOTO LIBRARY 59 Suez Canal (Chris Coe), 85 Old Cataract Pullman,
110 Belly Dancer, 117 Cairo–Aswân Express (Rick Strange).

J ALLAN CASH PHOTOLIBRARY 27 Egyptian Antiquities Museum, 28 Head of
Ramses II, 37 Market, 94/5 Elephantine Island, 107 Luxor bazaar, 108 Street
market, 109 Winter Palace Hotel.

P CORY 25 Al Azhar Mosque, 113 Aswân, 123 Nile cruise, 124 Temple of
Karnak.

EGYPTIAN TOURIST OFFICE 66 St Catherine's Monastery.

MARY EVANS PICTURE LIBRARY 11 Bombardment of Alexandria, 19 Nubian
chiefs.

INTERNATIONAL PHOTOBANK 12 Sphinx, 35 Marriott Hotel, 42 Sphinx &
pyramids, 75 Luxor temple, 79 Colossi of Memnon, 81 Edfu.

NATURE PHOTOGRAPHERS LTD 88/9 Spiny-tailed lizard, 91 Desert locust
(S C Bisserot), 90/1 Egyptian geese (M Gore), 93 Hooded wheatear
(H Muller), 95 Chiffchaff (M Bolton), 97 Plover (K Carlson), 98 Painted lady
(P Sterry), 100 Sand partridge (R Tidman), 101 Egyptian vulture
(C Gomersall), 102/3 Sabre squirrel fish (D Smith).

A NELSON 6 Engraving Colossi of Memnon, 114 Camel trek.

C OSBORNE 31 Ibn Tulun Mosque, 98/9 Western Desert, 104 Sweetmeats,
105 Eating out.

SPECTRUM COLOUR LIBRARY 9 Tutankhamun Mask, 22 View of Cairo, 29
Rahotep & Nefret, 32 Mohammed Ali Mosque, 37 Souvenirs, 39 Sunset, 40/1
Pharaonic Village, 45 Ramses II, 46/7 Step Pyramid, 50 Alexandria, 57 British
war cemetery, 62 Ismailia mosque, 64/5 Sinai, 68/9 Nile Tours, 71 Temple of
Seti, 73 Dendera, 77 Temple of Karnak, 83 Abu Simbel, 86 Kom Ombo, 92/3
Feluccas on the Nile, 116 Bus Station, 120/1 Sunset, 122 Post boxes.

ZEFA PICTURES LTD Cover Pyramids & camel, 54 Qaytbay Fort, 61 Port Said.

Author's acknowledgements
The author gratefully acknowledges the assistance of the Egyptian State
Tourist Office in producing information and checking some facts during the
preparation of this book. Thanks are also due to Dr Yetia Saad for help with
phonetics.